Become the Most Important Person in the Room

YOUR 30-DAY PLAN FOR EMPATH EMPOWERMENT

ROSE ROSETREE

Women's Intuition Worldwide

Publisher's Cataloging-In-Publication Data
(Prepared by The Donohue Group, Inc.)

Rosetree, Rose.
   Become the most important person in the room : your 30-day plan for empath empowerment / by Rose Rosetree ; illustrations by Melanie Matheson and Meike Müller.

   p. : ill. ; cm.

Includes index.
   ISBN-13: 978-0-9752538-7-8
   ISBN-10: 0-9752538-7-5

1. Empathy. 2. Intuition. 3. Sensitivity (Personality trait) 4. Self-actualization (Psychology) 5. Aura. 6. Spiritual life—New Age movement. 7. Self-help techniques. I. Matheson, Melanie. II. Müller, Meike. III. Title.

BF575.E55 R674 2009
158.2

For **workshops, personal consultations, quantity discounts** or
foreign rights sales, email rights@rose-rosetree.com, call
703-404-4357, or write to Women's Intuition Worldwide, LLC,
116 Hillsdale Drive, Sterling, VA 20164.
Interact at www.rose-rosetree.com/blog.

Dedication

First there is a mountain.
Then there is no mountain.
Then there is.

So goes a great Buddhist saying. Really, this could be the theme song for any spiritual path that changes lives. Once you decide to experience a closer connection to God, guaranteed, your reality will be shaken, maybe turned inside out. Eventually, that reality will settle back to what it was before, only better.

Now, becoming a Skilled Empath isn't the same thing as mastering Buddhism or any other religion. Still it counts as a big deal. Do this book right and your reality will be turned inside out, guaranteed. Specifically, you will be turning your reality *right* side out. Keep in mind, nothing about the journey we're taking must involve big external drama, only a gentle and private sorting-out process.

I call this Empath Empowerment. It's a set of skills that you can learn easily, one chapter per day. Our 30-Day Plan for Empath Empowerment is designed to take you through these changes:

- Part One: When you have talent (but little skill) as an empath, *others* are The Most Important Person in The Room.
- Part Two: Developing skill, *you* become The Most Important Person in The Room.
- Part Three: Although you're still The Most Important Person in The Room, you can recognize other people with as much clarity as you wish.

You can help them more, yet stay free of their pain. Even in the midst of a crowd, *you can be yourself* fully… easily… consistently. That's being a Skilled Empath.

Hmm, are you wondering what it will feel like? Because the results will be so personal, your best preview of what to expect will come by answering these questions:

- How intense is my inner experience right now?
- How big an impression do I make in the outer world right now?
- Would I like to be considered as strong on the outside as I am on the inside? (Depending on how life shows up for you now, you might want to substitute other words for "strong," such as passionate, interesting, respect-worthy, wise.)

In addition to all you can gain in these ways, Empath Empowerment offers the prospect of a wonderful kind of loss. Wouldn't it be helpful if you could stop picking up other people's pain, fear, sadness, etc.?

Unskilled empaths do that constantly. Would you prefer to help others without paying a huge personal cost? That alone could be reason enough to become a Skilled Empath.

Now isn't too early to think about your goals for our 30-Day Plan. Would that include a deep kind of healing? Or could the skill set I teach you actually help for living "shallower"? Could skill help you become more joyful, powerful, helpful to others, secure in yourself?

What, exactly, will happen when you have gained Empath Empowerment? Come, find out.

Contents

Techniques

Your 30-Day Plan contains a number of techniques developed expressly for Empath Empowerment. They're listed here with page numbers for easy reference. But first, please note the following tips.

- For best results with all these techniques, keep things simple. Do each technique only, adding nothing, subtracting nothing... texting nothing.
- Sometimes one of my techniques may remind you of another technique you learned elsewhere. Don't substitute. Neither of us knows for sure what the effect would be, whereas all the techniques in this book have been developed and researched as part of a well tested system, Empath Empowerment.
- What if you feel the need to heal something in the midst of doing a technique? Don't. Mixing in other skill sets, like Reiki or E.F.T., may interfere with that particular technique's effectiveness. If you're going to do healing techniques, do them separately and afterwards.
- Giving yourself a hard time is never required. I can tell you in advance, none of my techniques contains a secret message like "Stop thinking" or "Become an entirely different person."

- Funny thing about the techniques in this book... they won't bring you results unless you actually do them.

Sometimes a reader will want to go through a self-help book without trying any techniques at all, just to get an overview. That's smart.

Afterwards, though, go back and try the techniques and assignments. Otherwise, you'll only gain concepts.

Concepts alone won't make you a Skilled Empath. And that would be such a waste. Our very simple techniques and assignments can change your life enormously for the better.

Meet Our Cast of Characters

This book is about you and how you manage to stay yourself while with other people. Unfortunately, I wasn't able to take your picture, posed gorgeously along with your best buds. Instead I substituted this crew. They're good sports who graciously consented to be in our photographs for this book.

More of them are empaths than you would find in a typical group. (If you had a larger statistical sample, you'd find that only 1 in 20 people is wired as an empath.)

Since I'll refer to our cast of characters throughout this book, they're introduced to you here with their names, plus whether or not they are empaths.

Wouldn't it be convenient if empaths and non-empaths were labeled this neatly in real life? Unfortunately, my labeling powers don't extend that far.

The trickiest caption in the picture says "You." This woman is a poor stand-in, I know. Especially if you're a guy. Please, imagine that our "You" looks exactly like the real you, and with an extremely flattering camera angle.

Note that everything in this book concerning our cast of characters (names, inside info. about their grooming products, etc.) is completely fictitious. In addition, fictitious names are used for every anecdote in this book. My clients and students deserve their privacy, after all. Their stories — mostly of not-yet-skilled empaths — are all too true.

Cast of Characters

An Unskilled Empath Among Friends

PART ONE:
Change
What Needs Changing

When you have talent (but little skill) as an empath, *others* can seem like The Most Important Person in The Room.

The nine people pictured here were at a party. Someone brought them together for a quick photo. Say that you're the one in the front row, that gray-ed out person.

Why are "You" looking grayed-out? That's what unskilled empaths tend to do without realizing it. Everybody but you seems more vivid. To yourself, it's as if you're pictured in lighter shades of gray.

Even if you worry about seeming "selfish" sometimes, you still could be putting yourself last. Part One will help to you find out for sure. Then I'll help you to change what needs changing.

True Empath Empowerment doesn't happen instantly. But our 30-Day Plan should do it for you... learning quite easily... one day at a time.

Day 1. Get the Picture

Digital cameras today are pretty advanced. Even so, they can't show what happens deep inside a person. The picture on Page xii is my attempt to remedy that. I've supplied a thrillingly accurate, split-second portrait of the inner you... as a not-yet-skilled empath.

What is happening inside you? I'm asking about your spiritual consciousness, the part of you that's awake inside.

Let's put that question in a more practical way. *"When you spend time with others, who gets to be The Most Important Person in The Room?"*

Until you become skilled as an empath, the answer probably varies from minute to minute, except for one thing. One person is consistently ignored, underplayed, de-emphasized, under-appreciated: You.

Sure, you'll have an overall sense of self. Outwardly, you may seem just like all the non-empaths in the room, walking and talking and chatting away in Elvish. (Okay, nobody in the room speaks Elvish, empath or not. Although our 30-Day Plan is seriously helpful, I reserve the right to make jokes.)

What is so different about your experience, just because you're an empath? There's an energy awareness of others, a subtext, like watching a TV show where little icons and news-flashes keep popping up at the edges of the screen.

Here are hypothetical examples of those flashy little attention-grabbers. Say that you are visiting with the cast of characters on our book's cover photo. All these folks are at a party with you.

Minutes ago, someone has brought you together for the group picture. Afterwards, everybody goes back to partying. What do you notice about them energetically?

ROSCOE, the older guy, dominates the conversation. You feel his energy bouncing off people, large as life and twice as bossy. You notice how others respond to him. Some are starting to feel pretty bad about themselves, the way Roscoe casually disrespects them. Each time this happens, you wish the person didn't feel so bad.

Eventually Roscoe turns his attention to you. On the surface, he could be acting perfectly nice. Yet intuitively you sense that he doesn't respect you as an equal. What then? He seems to view you like an unimpressive 10-year-old, none too bright, somebody who mistakenly wandered into this party to watch the grownups.

How you wish that Roscoe would acknowledge you properly. (For one thing, you *are* a grownup now, thank you.) Yet the more you react against Roscoe's image of you, the more you find yourself dumbing down into what he expects. It's like being a chameleon, only scarier.

HANNAH is involved in a friendly, animated conversation. Except, oops, her back sure seems to be hurting like crazy. And she seems anxious, too. Although Hannah hides the discomfort well, somehow you know. If only she felt better!

This wish is made so quickly, you don't consciously remember making it. Consequences follow anyway. (The technical term is "Taking on someone else's STUFF." We'll discuss that, and how to prevent it, later.)

Meanwhile, LEXI, that gorgeous young woman over in the corner, is clearly flirting with James. Wouldn't it be great if you could just enjoy how beautifully she's dressed? Behold that perfect jewelry.

Even her artless little tee shirt costs about five times as much as anything you own.

Behold and admire… except that will be hard. Beneath her charming smile, Lexi is also wearing the most annoying, smug air of superiority. What's with that? Exhausting!

As for JAMES, he seems pleasant enough. But omigosh, he is lusting after Lexi in the most obvious and embarrassing way. Obvious and embarrassing to you, that is.

Outwardly, James may be having a perfectly innocent conversation. He's not even staring, especially. Yet to you, the heat waves are so strong it's amazing that nobody else seems to notice. Even Lexi doesn't quite seem to notice, not at first.

As the sexual charge builds between James and Lexi, there's nothing you can do except, perhaps, try to avoid this tropical corner of the party.

When you're an unskilled empath, other people in the room can seem way more vivid than you. Is it common for you to have one or more of the following experiences while you're with others?

+ Wondering what it is like to be someone else.
+ Experiencing at depth what it feels like to be that person.
+ Finding problems, pain or fears, in others.
+ Wishing that things could be better for that other person.
+ Wishing that somehow you could help.
+ Observing anyone's conversation (even if it isn't yours), you automatically notice what's going on beneath the surface.
+ When someone has a negative judgment of you, it may be seem overwhelmingly obvious, no more a secret than if he or she started singing "La Bamba" in a very loud voice.
+ You might even slide into *acting* differently, more like the way you're expected to act.
+ Come to think of it, you may define yourself in that room as a bat would. Why? You're doing a human version of echolocation. Depending on how you sound to others, that's how you find yourself.

SOME PARTY

And I called this "a party"? Ouch.

If you're an unskilled empath, the other people in the room are in color, while you're more like black-and-white.

Doesn't everybody do that? Not really. Non-empaths naturally put themselves first. They experience *themselves* in vivid color, more than everyone else. A non-empath might occasionally have an insight, such as "I notice things going on beneath the surface of the conversation." But an empath has those insights constantly.

A Skilled Empath gets to be in full color, just like everyone else.

The simplest way to understand what it means to be a Skilled Empath is that you learn to make yourself The Most Important Person in The Room. Non-empaths do this from birth. They will always be able do this *more easily* than you. But that doesn't mean they will always do it *better*.

Consider this possibility. Despite not automatically being The Most Important Person in The Room, you have something else that is very valuable. You have at least one important gift as an empath. And that gift is trainable. (Gifts will be discussed in more detail tomorrow.)

When you learn how to use your gift(s) on purpose, your quality of life can improve dramatically, compared to what you have now.

The Most Important Person in The Room — you can definitely feel that way (sanely) by becoming a Skilled Empath.

But getting the full skill set in place takes a 30-Day Plan for Empath Empowerment, not a 10-second summary.

For a preview, take some Random Snapshots.

Random Snapshots

What does it mean, feeling and acting like The Most Important Person in The Room?

To breathe life into the concept, try the technique I call "Random Snapshots. You can do it whenever two or more people are near you, interacting together.

Observe family, friends, business associates, even strangers — anyone in a room with you and at least two other person. Focus on one of these people at a time. (For this technique, we'll call everyone else but you by the same name, "Pat.")

Observe Pat's body language and expression or just get a vibe. You're not doing hard science here, but noticing in whatever ways come naturally.

Based on what you observe, does Pat feel like The Most Important Person in The Room?

Everyone has the right to feel like The Most Important Person in The Room. Yet not everyone claims that right.

Does Pat seem self-absorbed? That's no insult necessarily. A person can act very politely while being self-absorbed. In fact, a common synonym for that is "self-confident."

YOUR ASSIGNMENT FOR DAY 1

Brave Explorer, your assignment is simple. As you deal with people today, take the occasional Random Snapshot with your awareness. Who shows the kind of confidence that suggests feeling like The Most Important Person in The Room?

Within the next 24 hours, will you encounter a single person who can be deeply aware of others (as you naturally are) yet who also shows full self-confidence?

Such a person would be a role model for you, a Skilled Empath.

Skilled Empaths are rare… so far. In 30 days, *you* can become one of them. Don't let the scarcity of role models bother you. Call what you're doing "leadership."

Day 2. Take This Quiz

Are you an empath? If so, what is your gift? Take this Empath Awareness Quiz to find out.

Having even one gift would qualify you as a card-carrying empath, with all the rights and privileges to which membership entitles you. Do you have several gifts, just one, or none? By reading the following descriptions, you may relate or not. Answer YES or NO, depending.

I should confess that I have mixed in some descriptions that aren't about being an empath at all. Instead they are popular misunderstandings about being an empath. Even if you are so sophisticated as an empath that you can instantly spot the trick questions, answer them anyway: If you can relate to the statment, answer YES. If not, answer NO.

EMPATH AWARENESS QUIZ

Can you relate, YES or NO?

1. I can catch another person's mood as easily as if I'm catching a yawn.

2. Although I don't feel other people's feelings, I sure know what those feelings are. For instance, I might know that the other person is lying, or clueless, or feeling five different things all at once.

3. Much of the time, I feel lost and alone, sometimes even miserable.

4. I can always tell if a woman is promiscuous, even if she's nicely dressed.

5. When I hike in a forest and the trees or animals are suffering, I can feel it.

6. I might actually be part chameleon, because I talk differently with different people, using bigger words or smaller. I'll give different examples, depending. Like when I'm with an artist, colors seem brighter. With a musician, I notice sounds more than usual.

7. Back at catching things, I have been known to catch other people's headaches or other physical symptoms. I guess I'm suggestible. Could I even be a hypochondriac?

8. I don't necessarily catch other people's aches and pains but I can be with someone and start feeling pressure or pain in different parts of my body.

9. I might have a selfish version of this. Nothing happens in my own body but I'll be pretty sure, sometimes, that another person is tired or hurts somewhere physically.

10. Sometimes I can tell things about people spiritually without having to ask, e.g., A person has something to prove spiritually, or hates the subject of religion, or has a strong spiritual connection.

11. I love fantasy novels, so naturally I'm intrigued when I see people describing themselves as a Fallen Angel Empath or an Artist Empath (where "Everything you touch turns to song and is freed by the color of your eyes.") When I find words like these on the Internet, I could read for hours. I wonder if I could be all these different types of empath.

12. I'll be with someone and suddenly I'll be like, "Life is good." or "Life is bad." Feelings like this can just flicker through me, depending on whom I'm with. Another weird one is that, out of nowhere, I might have the feeling "God loves me." or "God is scary."

This happens all on its own. Nobody around me is having some "big, serious conversation about what I believe." I just have these random experiences in the back of my mind. Could that happen because I am some kind of empath?

13. Talk about discomfort, un-watered plants drive me crazy. I can practically hear them scream.

14. It bothers me when people mistreat machines, like computers or cars. People think nothing of forcing the machines, kicking them, calling them names. This upsets me, even if I don't own the machine and won't have to pay for fixing it later.

15. Caring is the sign of an empath, isn't it? When I always root for the underdog and cry when I watch movies, what kind of empath does that make me?

16. I'm really good at Emotional Intelligence. I can label anger, sadness, rage, happiness, etc., whether it belongs to me or not. Which empath ability makes me so good at this?

17. Dysfunctional patterns learned during childhood have caused me to anticipate what other people need.

18. Holding a crystal is magical for me; the same thing with precious gemstones. They take me on an energy ride, showing me different ways to be.

19. Body language tells me everything I need to know. Anyone talented like me finds it very easy to figure out from expression if somebody likes you, is a bad person, etc. In five seconds, I can learn everything that matters.

20. I'm just glad people wear different clothes from each other. Otherwise, I'd have a really hard time telling them apart.

QUIZ ANSWERS

1. I can catch another person's mood as easily as if I'm catching a yawn.

YES, Emotional Oneness is my name for that gift. I'm delighted to learn that you are a fellow sufferer. Kidding about the suffering part. This is a wonderful empath gift, no weirder than any of the others. With all empath gifts, once you get skills you can help other people elegantly, and without suffering.

2. Although I don't feel other people's feelings, I sure know what those feelings are. For instance, I might know that the other person is lying, or clueless, or feeling five different things all at once.

YES, you have Emotional Intuition, a gift for appreciating people's emotions at a distance. Ever wonder how people can get away with lying to others about emotions? Not everyone — not even every empath — has Emotional Intuition or Emotional Oneness.

3. Much of the time, I feel lost and alone, sometimes even miserable.

NO. Being an empath need not involve misery. Even being an *unskilled empath* doesn't necessarily involve misery; it's just that your life can improve a lot once you become skilled. Maybe this book will take you from *pretty happy* to *outrageously happy.*

By contrast, you could be miserable for reasons that have nothing at all to do with being an empath, like puberty or having a bad hair day.

4. I can always tell if a woman is promiscuous, even if she's nicely dressed.

NO, sorry, this isn't necessarily about being an empath, either. It could be a matter of psychological projection. If you specialize in noticing a particular kind of problem in others, you may have some unfinished business.

And if you are "always" running into people with a particular kind of sexual problem or anger management issues, control issues, narcissism, etc., I would definitely encourage you to seek help from a mental health professional.

5. When I hike in a forest and the trees or animals are suffering, I can feel it.

YES, you are an Environmental Empath if you notice the beauty or suffering — or just plain specialness — of a forest.

As this type of empath, you'll feel quite different at the beach, in the desert, or pounding pavement in a big city. I don't mean having varied experiences depending on whether you're a news reporter or mortician but, rather, an inner quality that shifts.

Your thinking could be subtly different, or different environments could alter how you feel in your body, how you walk, or what you hear in the silence around you.

Also, YES, you are Animal Empath if sometimes you connect to the inner world of animals. This could happen with all God's creatures or just one particular kind of animal, like ferrets.

Animal Empaths know that each animal or pet has a distinctive way to be. With this gift, you appreciate the animal's experience on a deep level, like knowing when your favorite ferret is excited, frightened or joyful. As an empath, you're not just observing behavior from the outside but connecting intuitively to something deeper.

6. I might actually be part chameleon, because I talk differently with different people, using bigger words or smaller. I'll give different examples, depending. Like when I'm with an artist, colors seem brighter. With a musician, I notice sounds more than usual.

YES, you have described the gift (and challenge) of being an Intellectual Empath. Intuitively you understand how different people think — not reading specific thoughts in their minds but sensing how to reach that person best. Until skilled, you may feel like a chameleon but, trust me, you are no reptile.

7. Back at catching things, I have been known to catch other people's headaches or other physical symptoms. I guess I'm suggestible. Could I even be a hypochondriac?

YES, you are a Messy, Suggestible, Hypochondriacal Empath. Wait, that's not my official name for this gift. I call it Physical Oneness. Once you are skilled, it's a very valuable gift, being able to experience other people's problems in your own body. Wait and see.

8. I don't necessarily catch other people's aches and pains but I can be with someone and start feeling pressure or pain in different parts of my body.

YES, this also counts as an empath gift. It is the gift I just called Physical Oneness. Some empaths receive information about others in the form of direct physical sensations, but not always. This isn't necessarily a one-on-one equation, like "her stomachache = my stomachache." It could be more like "her worrying = my stomachache."

As a Skilled Empath, you'll learn to interpret these symbolic physical experiences, finding out what the true message is.

You'll also learn how to avoid taking on information just because you happen to be near somebody who feels bad. What a relief, turning your gifts OFF or ON purposely! After all, how busy do you want your body to be? Wouldn't it be nice to just feel normal (whatever that is for you)?

9. I might have a selfish version of this. Nothing happens in my own body but I'll be pretty sure, sometimes, that another person is tired or hurts somewhere physically.

YES, only don't call this gift "Selfish Empathy" because you can help people with it, just like any other empath gift. Instead, call this gift Physical Intuition.

The name means that you know what is happening to other people's bodies. You happen to receive this information at a distance, rather than downloading the data directly through sensations in your own personal body.

10. Sometimes I can tell things about people spiritually without having to ask, e.g., A person has something to prove spiritually, or hates the subject of religion, or has a strong spiritual connection.

YES, count this as Spiritual Intuition. The jumping-off-point could be as simple as looking at the person's forehead or hearing his/her voice. Of course, this knowledge about religion would be something other than empath talent if the person happens to be wearing a very large cross or a turban.

11. I love fantasy novels, so naturally I'm intrigued when I see people describing themselves as a Fallen Angel Empath or an Artist Empath (where "Everything you touch turns to song and is freed by the color of your eyes.") When I find words like these on the Internet, I could read for hours. I wonder if I could be all these different types of empath.

NO, because having an interest in colorful names like these involves fantasy fiction more than being an honest-to-goodness empath with real-life experiences.

It's not about being an empath if you are fascinated by horses or spaceships or brown paper packages tied up with string. Nothing about your lifestyle reveals whether or not you are an empath.

12. I'll be with someone and suddenly I'll be like, "Life is good." or "Life is bad." Feelings like this can just flicker through me, depending on whom I'm with. Another weird one is that, out of nowhere, I might have the feeling "God loves me." or "God is scary." This happens all on its own. Nobody around me is having some "big, serious conversation about what I believe." I just have these random experiences in the back of my mind. Could that happen because I am some kind of empath?

YES. Good catch! This is Spiritual Oneness. In the past you may not always have connected these subtle inner experiences to the people they came from. A Skilled Empath would. In fact, as a Skilled Empath, you can also stop having random experiences like these. Unskilled Spiritual Oneness can cause a deep kind of anxiety that is hard to shake until you get skills.

13. Talk about discomfort, un-watered plants drive me crazy. I can practically hear them scream.

YES, you're a Plant Empath. This gift could help you to garden… or cook.

14. It bothers me when people mistreat machines, like computers or cars. People think nothing of forcing the machines, kicking them, calling them names. This upsets me, even if I don't own the machine and won't have to pay for fixing it later.

YES, count this as being a Mechanical Empath (when you care about the machine, not when you do the kicking). Every machine contains its own consciousness, and it may even have its own deva, an elemental intelligence assigned to it.

As a Mechanical Empath, you can move into the consciousness of that machine. Intuitively you know what will fix it. With skill, the problems of machines will stop feeling like your personal problems.

15. Caring is the sign of an empath, isn't it? When I always root for the underdog and cry when I watch movies, what kind of empath does that make me?

NO, caring and crying can happen for many reasons. An empath moves in and out of the direct experience of what it is like to be someone else. This can be quite subtle, and it need not involve drama of any kind.

16. I'm really good at Emotional Intelligence. I can label anger, sadness, rage, happiness, etc., whether it belongs to me or not. Which empath ability makes me so good at this?

Congratulations but NO, being good at Emotional Intelligence doesn't bear any relationship to being an empath. Anyone can learn the skill set of Emotional Intelligence, but that won't solve an empath's biggest problem, which is the need to remove pain belonging to others from your aura.

17. Dysfunctional patterns learned during childhood have caused me to anticipate what other people need.

NO, this has nothing to do with being an empath, either. Here's the only connection: If you were born as an empath, you learned to anticipate at greater depth than a non-empath.

Let's clear up a popular misunderstanding. Empath abilities are not dysfunctional patterns, nor are they learned.

Instead, being an empath shows in your aura right from the time you're in the womb. I'm not joking. You can check this out for yourself, since everyone (empath or not) can learn to read auras.

With that skill set, try reading auras of pregnant women, in person or from photos, separating out the information belonging to mother and child, or mother and twins. Every human being has a very distinctive energy field, and it's filled with information. Some of this changes, some doesn't.

I can teach you to read auras, whatever the horrors or joys of your childhood. I can teach you to develop Emotional Intelligence. But I cannot make you into an empath.

18. Holding a crystal is magical for me; the same thing with precious gemstones. They take me on an energy ride, showing me different ways to be.

YES, you're a Crystal Empath. Gemstones carry fascinating energy properties. With this gift, you'll experience a shift in consciousness just by picking up the stone, closing your eyes, and paying attention to what happens next.

Incidentally, this form of intuitive travel has nothing to do with whether you like reading books about the energy properties of different crystals.

19. Body language tells me everything I need to know. Anyone talented like me finds it very easy to figure out from expression if somebody likes you, is a bad person, etc. In five seconds, I can learn everything that matters.

NO, sorry, this is not the gift of an empath. Certainty that you instantly know everything about another person is actually the opposite. Empaths tend to be explorers, not stereotypers.

One way to see what I mean by this is to peek ahead at Day 23 and "Body Language Turned Inside Out." You'll enjoy this chapter whether you are an empath or not.

20. I'm just glad people wear different clothes from each other. Otherwise, I'd have a really hard time telling them apart.

NO, you're probably not an empath of any kind. But you might have a bright future as a fashion designer.

CONGRATULATIONS

How did you score? Even one gift as an empath qualifies you as a card-carrying empath.

So, what else do you need to know right away?

That card is invisible.

You have the right to remain silent. Anything you say can and will be used against you — wait, those are Miranda Rights that a police officer will read before carrying you away.

Empath Rights are just the same as anyone else's, including free will, the pursuit of God and happiness, seeking a good life the best way you know.

For you, becoming a Skilled Empath might just turn out to be one of those ways.

YOUR ASSIGNMENT FOR DAY 2

Brave Explorer, think about your gift(s) as an empath. Do you notice anyone else who seems to have the same gift(s) as you? What about friends of yours who might have different empath gifts?

Educate them, if you wish. Probably they have never discussed what it means to be an empath. Or they think that "empath" always means "taking on other people's emotions." Yet one more misunderstanding that is common among beginners! Most empath gifts aren't about emotions at all. Play around with all these cool new names:

- Animal Empath
- Crystal Empath
- Emotional Intuition
- Emotional Oneness
- Environmental Empath
- Intellectual Empath
- Mechanical Empath
- Physical Intuition
- Physical Oneness
- Plant Empath
- Spiritual Intuition
- Spiritual Oneness

These names will come in handy, starting with what we explore to-morrow. Remember, if you have even one of these gifts, that qualifies you to consider yourself an empath. Whatever the gift, *an empath has a gift for directly experiencing what it is like to be someone else.*

That's what it means. That simple. That fascinating.

Day 3. Be Deep, Sometimes

Here's your chance to show the world you are truly a deep person. Depth is reason enough for you to be recognized as The Most Important Person in The Room. So let's all join hands and yell, to the count of three, "I'm deeply profound, not shallow."

Wait, that won't work, will it? Consider:

1. Deep people don't need to do things like cheerleading in order to prove they are deep. To be "deep" means that you go within, rather than taking your cues from others. Really, for human life, the opposite of "deep" isn't shallow. It's "wide," as in social and friendly and connected to the world outside of your inner self.

2. You don't become The Most Important Person in The Room by asking anyone else for permission, recognition, etc.

3. Deep people don't just do things like follow someone else's command to join hands with other people and yell. First you want to know why.

So let's clear up this social thing once and for all. To become skilled as an empath, you don't need to show the world anything. Empath Empowerment isn't about personal image, like whether or not you dress with attitude. Being skilled as an empath doesn't hinge on social choices of any kind.

How do I know? Surveys, for one thing. Wherever in the world I teach Empath Empowerment, I'll conduct the following survey. Let's try it now.

Boundary Survey

Raise your hand if:

- You have tried to tighten up your boundaries with other people.
- You have tried to stop being overly sensitive.
- You have attempted to visualize a mirror or façade or bubble – any kind of invisible shield.
- You have tried to protect yourself by avoiding people who drain energy, like narcissists and psychic vampires.

This far into the Survey, I find that most people's hands go up. Has yours? To continue:

- Now, raise your other hand if this has helped you much.

Usually, very few hands go up.

Of course, everyone *wants* to raise hands. Hardworking empaths don't want to feel as though they have failed. It's especially humiliating not to raise your hand because "everyone knows" that socially-based approaches, like "boundaries," represent your only hope for a balanced life.

Wrong. They aren't the only hope. And for reasons you'll soon understand, those boundary-based approaches aren't even a good hope. Boundary-type approaches don't work very well. Not for empaths, anyway.

Brave Explorer, I'm going to teach you how to *use the power of your consciousness* to become a Skilled Empath.

In my experience, this is the only approach that really works. What do the contrasting approaches in our Boundary Survey have in common? They're social.

That means wide, not deep.

What does it mean to be an empath, anyway? Unlike non-empaths, since birth you have journeyed in consciousness, tripping in and out of other people's auras.

Is this done consciously? Not when you're *unskilled*. Which is why I call this kind of journeying "unskilled Empath Merge."

The travel isn't done slowly and deliberately, like planning a trip to Disney World. Nonetheless, as an empath you're wired to make super-quick, super-deep journeys in consciousness. Unskilled Empath Merges happen spontaneously, and at random, from birth.

The learning part is lovely, and you may also be helping people with every journey (although at a high personal cost). But there's one problem, for sure. With every unskilled Empath Merge, you'll pick up STUFF from the other person. It will move from that other person's aura into your own.

Unskilled Empath Merges happen at a different frequency from social behavior. Being with other people, working hard to firm up your boundaries, what's to keep your aura from spreading out into an un-skilled Empath Merge? Nothing.

Socially-based approaches aren't bad, but they work much better for non-empaths, the ones who don't pop in and out of other people's auras by means of consciousness. Ironic, isn't it?

Today's project is to start claiming the power of your consciousness. This power was always available, if only you knew how to use it.

Be Deep

Here is an exercise to activate the power of your consciousness. (Please, if you are just leafing through the book and don't plan to actually do the exercise yet, skip immediately to the next chapter. This exercise is for doing, not skimming.)

Read through the following points. Then do them, taking the occasional peek as needed.

Close the door. Do whatever it takes to be alone without anyone else clamoring for your attention. Turn off the background music, your computer and all those other electronic companions.

Elvis will have to leave the building. (Meanwhile, turn off his cell.)

1. Sit comfortably. Uncross your legs or arms or any other place you are pretzeling. Put out your cigarette. Park your gum. You're gonna go deep, and go it alone. Woo-hoo!
2. Close your eyes for about 10 seconds.
3. Open your eyes.
4. Close your eyes for about 20 seconds.
5. Open your eyes.
6. Close your eyes for about 30 seconds.
7. Open your eyes.

You're done for now, so let's compare notes.

DEEP? WHATEVER

Think about what just happened while your eyes were closed. This wasn't a wildly dramatic experience, was it? What matters is that, whatever happened, you were experiencing it with your *consciousness* — the part of you that keeps awake deep inside.

With eyes closed, you could have noticed thoughts, sounds, emotions, physical sensations. You could have heard words in your head, seen colors or images. You could have felt space or heard silence, heard space or felt silence.

To use a technical term, we can call any of these experiences "whatever."

Any whatever would be fine. You could even have had more than one whatever at a time.

Consciousness lies beneath every whatever, just as this page you're reading contains words printed on it and blank space beneath. We need that blank space in order to see the words. Similarly, we need consciousness inside to be able to notice every passing thought, sound, emotion, etc.

Did you notice how easily you could have your eyes closed and notice things? Effort isn't necessary for an experience to count. Neither is drama.

It isn't as though *nothing* happens with your eyes closed unless you see a tall, skinny guy with purple hair and black clothes, a clueless sort of person who rides his skateboard really fast and then crashes into you. *Consciousness is subtle.*

Back at our previous exercise, trying hard is the only way you could have messed it up. If that happened, your "punishment" is to do the exercise again, only relax this time.

Repeat Be Deep if:

- You were struggling for inner drama like a close encounter with the crashing skateboard guy,
- Or you blamed yourself for having thoughts
- Or you gave yourself a headache due to trying so hard
- Or you tried sneaking in other techniques you have learned because you couldn't stand going for three seconds naked in consciousness without dressing yourself up in something extra-flashy.

Go back, Brave Explorer. Dare to be simple and do our Be Deep exercise once more. And when you have managed to do the simple, sloppy, effortless technique, such as it is....

HELLO

Imagine a fairy tale where the Great Flying Turkey (or some other being of enormous spiritual power and compassion) has just touched you with his magic wand, awakening you from The Enchantment.

Ta da!

Using Be Deep, you have done the magic act on your own. You have reminded your conscious mind that your consciousness is *you*. I mean a deep down version of you, independent of any social situation.

This version of you isn't obvious but subtle. You may not feel absolutely convinced that you have had "an experience" in the way you would if, for instance, you had just been run over by a truck.

That's a good thing, and I don't only mean the lack of tire tracks all over your body. For anything that I teach you, don't be sure. Be sloppy. Now you officially have permission.

If you already meditate, or pray powerfully, or read auras, you are familiar with using your consciousness on purpose in order to accomplish something. Becoming a Skilled Empath will also involve using your consciousness, but differently.

YOUR ASSIGNMENT FOR DAY 3

Today's assignment is to become more comfortable with your consciousness.

It's simple. It's deep. It requires no effort for you to notice it, merely a subtle shift of attention.

Once you're familiar with consciousness, shifting to an inner awareness is no harder than picking up a phone and saying, "Hello."

Brave Explorer, once you're familiar with consciousness, you can aim it in any direction you like. And, in future chapters, you'll be doing a lot more of that.

Does aiming your consciousness mean forcing or pushing? No way. It's simply being.

Let's review what makes non-doing, this simple thing, so important:

1. Turning your empath gifts OFF or ON effectively requires that you actively use your consciousness.
2. Avoiding toxic people isn't about consciousness. It's a social skill.
3. Firming up your boundaries with others, like refusing to buy candy bars for your neighbor or become her love slave — that isn't about consciousness either.
4. Only consciousness can keep you clear inside yourself and make you The Most Important Person in The Room.

With today's assignment, you'll do the Be Deep exercise at random intervals during the day until you feel comfortable with it. Either do the version we've covered so far or you use the version on the next page. The Be Deep Quickie will take even less time.

Be Deep Quickie

This is a super-fast way to become conscious of your consciousness.

1. Close your eyes for about 1 second.
2. Open your eyes.
3. Close your eyes for about 2 seconds.
4. Open your eyes.
5. Close your eyes for about 3 seconds.
6. Open your eyes.
7. Notice this: One thing has been the same whether your eyes were open or closed. You. Your inner consciousness has been there. It always will be there. That's the point!
8. Also notice: When your eyes are closed, consciousness is directed within. Many experiences are possible, such as thoughts, feelings, physical sensations. These "whatevers" happen effortlessly.

You can always choose to be conscious of your consciousness. You can notice whatevers as part of it. You can pay attention to consciousness now and forget about it later. No damage will result. Consciousness will be available for your notice whenever you *choose* to notice.

As a skilled empath, mostly you won't be paying attention to your consciousness. Occasionally you will make a subtle shift or two, then let go.

That occasional, effortless, expert tweak to your consciousness is the essence of Empath Empowerment. And Be Deep Quickie can help you to become familiar with this gigantic, free, inner resource.

Grab a Be Deep Quickie whenever you wish. Every time, always, for life… you have that wonderful inner resource called "consciousness."

Take five or more random breaks today to Be Deep, slow version or quick, as you wish. Tomorrow, we'll take your experience further.

Day 4. Delicious Bites

Brave Explorer, today you can do an easy version of something that diet experts recommend:

"Order that super-rich dessert. Take your first bite and stop to savor the taste. First bites are the most delicious part of any dessert. If you do it right, really tasting, one bite or two is all you need. Then you'll be perfectly satisfied."

Just a bite or two, right? Such a heroic idea! Unfortunately, if you're like me, in real life you'll settle for many additional bites, even if they don't taste quite so good as that first fork of fudge cake. Some of us (and I do mean me, here) just might stuff ourselves silly. Possibly we'll pack in those inferior bites until an entire cake is gone.

Certain life experiences are so gosh-darned delicious that it can be really hard to say "Stop. I enjoyed this, but enough is enough."

Shopping can be one of those experiences. So can video games. Admit it, you have certain favorite can't-stop activities in life. But did you ever think that empathic hitch-hiking might be one of them?

EMPATHIC HITCH-HIKING

It happens whenever an empath moves into the experience of being another person, pet, plant, etc. If you find cake hard to avoid, that's nothing compared to the strange escapist pleasure of spontaneous unskilled Empath Merge.

It happens so fast, the term "split second" is too slow. Divide one split second into a thousand "shards." One shard, that's how fast it happens.

During this shard of time, an unskilled empath spontaneously merges auras with someone — anyone — in the room. So long as you're an unskilled empath, this super-fast empathic hitch-hiking occurs whenever you're with people.

The good news is, you gain a deep knowledge of what it is like to be those people. The bad news? Knowledge is stored subconsciously, where it will do your conscious mind no good.

Worse, unskilled Empath Merge causes your aura to takes on some fear or pain that originally belonged to the other person. You bring back this STUFF (subconsciously, of course) as a kind of souvenir. There it stays indefinitely, stuck in your aura.

Remember our idea from Day 3? Empaths need to use consciousness to become skilled. So it isn't enough to adjust your social behavior. If you try hard to firm up your boundaries, you'll only manage to make nice firm boundaries. STUFF will enter regardless.

A skilled aura reader can tell the difference. Let's use the example of Hannah's aura. She has worked so hard at her boundaries that she has formed one wall around her Heart Chakra and two walls around her Solar Plexus Chakra.

The location and number of walls in an aura will depend on the ways that a person has worked to make her artificial boundaries.

Wherever they're located, Hannah's walls make it hard for her friends to get close to her. Meanwhile, those walls don't prevent Hannah from empathic hitch-hiking and picking up STUFF.

So that's why I'm teaching you Empath Empowerment skills based in consciousness, not changing outer behavior or creating visualizations that further clutter up an aura.

By taking more interest in yourself, you will gradually stop aura-level hitch-hiking, finding it more rewarding to drive your own car.

Can we stop here? Is it enough to intellectually understand the concept?

Sorry, no. You'll need to learn specific skills for using consciousness actively, paying prime quality attention to yourself. Let's start to build on what you did yesterday with Be Deep and the Be Deep Quickie.

Quality Time with Yourself

This simple technique can help you develop skill at directing your consciousness in a natural, effortless way. For just a few seconds:

1. Stop whatever you're doing.
2. Close your eyes.
3. And pay attention to whatever you happen to notice about yourself.

That's it, nothing fancy at all.

Notice? Quality Time With Yourself does not involve saying words like, "I'm being aware of myself." This isn't self-hypnosis. Instead you're tasting your own presence.

How will that taste?

- You might notice energy or silence.
- Or emotions. Or physical sensations.
- Or more than one thing. Maybe many things, all of them about you.
- If you happen to have a thought about someone or something other than yourself, that's okay. Just be more interested in whatever you notice about *you*.
- You might feel as if you are slowing time down just a bit.
- It could feel like "me time," because you are interested in something (anything) about yourself.

This moment of Quality Time With Yourself is mainly about being, not changing how you think, not improving yourself, not even doing anything in particular.

Don't worry about having some big, flashy mystical experience. Paying attention to yourself, with consciousness, is really quite ordinary.

If you have thoughts, that's okay. (Note: You're also allowed to have skin.)

YOUR ASSIGNMENT FOR DAY 4

Quality time isn't quantity time. So today's assignment won't take long.

To succeed at this exercise, all you will need is one minute's time to be aware of yourself. So how about doing that three different times today?

Quality Time With Yourself could be compared to having a few bites of delicious cake. Get the flavor of *you*, right now, right in the moment. Of course, you'll be tasting consciousness, not a crave-making, sweet-tooth-tickling dessert.

To become a Skilled Empath, you don't have to spend every waking moment gloating over your own consciousness. An occasional taste can be plenty, like that first bite of cake.

Day 5. Wakeup Call

"Operator, give me a wakeup call at 7:00 a.m."

Isn't that a delightful perk of staying in a hotel? I love being able to ask for that special help with getting up in the morning. Today, I'm going to teach you a way to wake up your inner self, effortlessly moving out STUFF that never really belonged to you, STUFF that sneaked in because you were a *talented* empath but not yet *skilled*.

First though, let's delve more thoroughly into how STUFF sneaks into an unskilled empath's aura. To illustrate my explanation, here are pictures of two people — "You" and Lexi – with auras included. Turn the page and you'll see them.

Note: I have smooshed both bodies and auras so they can fit into the space available. This is a symbolic illustration made for teaching purposes. No body parts have really been amputated.

THE HIGH-VIBE AURA OF AN EMPATH

At first glance, the auras belonging to Lexi and "You" might look identical. Except "You," on the left, are an empath.

The dotted line at the edge of your aura is meant to symbolize your ultra-refined, quick moving energy field. Compared to a non-empath, your entire aura has a relatively refined, porous texture, moving at a faster rate of vibration. All empaths have that kind of aura.

Lexi is the gal on the right, a non-empath, a.k.a. "normal person." Her aura is just as good, but not refined in this particular way, so no dotted line for her, just a regular line.

Take a look.

The High-Vibe Aura of an Empath

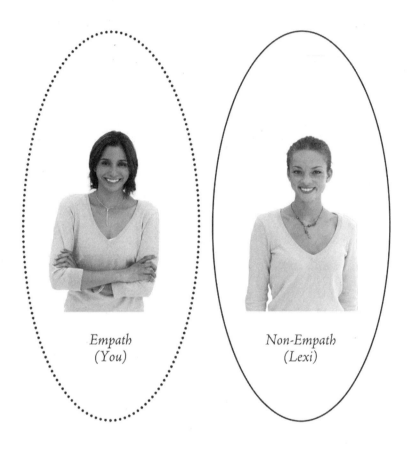

Empath
(You)

Non-Empath
(Lexi)

BASICS ABOUT AURAS AND "STUFF"

Just because you're doing our 30-Day Plan doesn't mean you know all about aura reading. So here are some basics you'll need to know as an empath.

Everyone's aura contains major chakras, centers of information that correspond to certain parts of your body, like Throat Chakra or Heart Chakra. One of my favorite discoveries after decades of teaching how to read auras is that each major chakra contains 50 different databanks of information; minor chakras have many databanks, too.

To picture all those databanks, think of a pipe organ, where every one of the 50 pipes can be a different size, play a different note.

Each databank contains two *types* of information. There will be a GIFT of your soul, something you can do beautifully. GIFTS in auras are permanent, no work involved, like having fingerprints. (Those include your empath gift(s), incidentally.)

Unfortunately, each aura databank can also show problems. This second type of information includes problems related to:

- Old traumas left over from childhood.
- New traumas, brought to you by the tooth fairy... or your ex, or your boss, or any tough relationship.
- Cords of attachment, e.g.., Energy tubes between your aura and the auras of all your significant others, structures that replay old patterns of pain 24/7 — like a nightmare MP3 file run amok.

You get the idea. I had to find a technical term for all these short-and long-term patterns that can clog up an aura. So I have chosen the term STUFF. At any given time, a person's aura will contain a combination of GIFTS of your soul and STUFF.

STUFF can always be healed. But that can take expert help, using technical skills from Energy Spirituality, Energy Medicine or Energy Psychology. Until it is healed, STUFF makes life much less fun.

In our diagram on the next page, the squiggles represent stored-up STUFF in both people's auras. Check it out.

STUFF in Auras

Empath
(You)

Non-Empath
(Lexi)

When you, a born empath, hang out with another person like Lexi, a kind of reflex action happens between your aura and hers. Your aura surrounds it, giving a kind of hug. As described yesterday, the technical term for this is an *unskilled Empath Merge.*

Remember how long that takes? Just one shard of time. So an unskilled Empath Merge isn't even conscious.

Nurturing, supporting, extending friendship or love, seeking understanding... ah, it's a beautiful thing. Except more than that happens, as you may already have guessed from our illustration on the facing page.

Automatically, after doing an unskilled Empath Merge, you will take some of that other person's STUFF back into your aura. Go ahead. Flip over to the next page and check out that illustration.

Oy veh! See what I mean about Empathic Hitch-Hiking?

If you look carefully, you'll see that Lexi's aura now contains less STUFF. Nice for her! Several squiggles of her STUFF (not all of them, but plenty) have gone into "Y*our*" aura.

In this series of illustrations, squiggles are drawn differently on "You" and Lexi just to clarify that concept. In reality, STUFF is blobby, some bits bigger and some bits smaller, and none quite so artistic looking as what has been shown here.

Attractively drawn or not, STUFF isn't lovely to wear inside your energy field. Frankly, the very idea of suck-in of other people's STUFF, whether nicely drawn or not, is....

JUST A BIT DISGUSTING

And it may not cheer you up to realize that all this has been happening throughout your entire life. Probably it has happened without your consciously noticing the aura dynamics, either. How come?

1. The process itself isn't conscious. Instead, it's on the level of auras and subconscious awareness.
2. No effort is required. Unskilled Empath Merges happen automatically.
3. And they happen really fast, in just one quick shard of time.

During an Unskilled Empath Merge

*Empath
(You)*

*Non-Empath
(Lexi)*

Before you began this 30-Day Plan, if you were wired as an empath and possessed merely talent, not skill, you couldn't keep this STUFF -slurping reflex from happening. It was automatic.

Okay, maybe you had noticed what was happening, in a way. Looking back, maybe you noticed that while you were in the room with Lexi, she seemed more vivid to you than... you. Later, after leaving the room, you might have felt drained.

What if a YouTube video had somehow captured the behavior of your aura during this visit? Here's what the viewers would see happening during your unskilled Empath Merge. During that shard of time:

1. Your aura expanded to surround the aura of the second person.
2. You pulled some of the other person's STUFF out of his/her aura and into yours.
3. The edges of your aura returned to normal, back to surrounding your body only.
4. And now the other person's aura contains less STUFF, while yours has more.

Unskilled Empath Merges represent a very sweet form of service to humanity. Doing these STUFF pickups could be considered the ultimate in selfless, heroic, incognito volunteer work.

Except how much does it really help the other person?

Lexi, for instance, may quickly replace the fear, anger, pain etc. that you lifted from her.

Why? She hasn't consciously chosen to heal or learn anything.

Meanwhile you, the empath, have done a good deed. But the long-term effect is to clog up your aura with STUFF. (Turn the page for a symbolic representation.)

Every bit of that STUFF causes suffering for you.

After an Unskilled Empath Merge

Empath
(You)

Non-Empath
(Lexi)

IS THAT FAIR?

Don't even ask. That is one useless question, on a par with asking, "But why does gravity have to point down?"

In our *next* chapter, I'll explain why I think all this happens. In *no* chapter of this book will I promise that life, short-term, is fair. But in *this* chapter I'm going to teach you the simplest thing you can do about the problem that we could call "When porous box contains other people's squiggles."

You see, what I've shown you with these diagrams is how an unskilled empath winds up picking up other people's STUFF. A fully Skilled Empath avoids picking up STUFF in the first place. So most of our 30-Day Plan will emphasize changing that habit.

Today's skill, however, can be a useful workaround. When you have picked up STUFF from an unintentional, unskilled Empath Merge, you can use a technique to help you get rid of that STUFF.

Brave Explorer, I call this technique "Wakeup Call" because it works like a wakeup call to your own aura:

"Hello!!! Dump out that extra STUFF. It never really belonged to you. It came from other people. Don't you have enough to do, healing your own STUFF? Lose the extra, already."

Yesterday's assignment, Quality Time With Yourself, helped you practice paying attention to yourself in a deep way, *using consciousness.* Be Deep and the Be Deep Quickie also have helped you to direct that consciousness toward yourself in a quality way.

Any such technique makes it easier to tell when you have been picking up STUFF from the likes of Lexi.

Talented or not, many unskilled empaths neglect themselves, routinely paying more attention — and better quality attention — to others.

Before becoming skilled, when they do get around to noticing themselves, many stay relatively superficial, emphasizing physical appearance or social dynamics.

How do most unskilled empaths approach "going inside, alone"? The closest they get might be seeing a reflection in a mirror... and even that face in the mirror may sometimes feel as if it belonged to a stranger.

Being empaths, however, we really can't afford to ignore ourselves. Paying just a bit of quality attention, even at random times during your day, will inform you when you're carrying STUFF. Even if you don't know for sure, at least, you'll get a hunch.

Whenever you suspect that STUFF belonging to others might have landed in your aura, do the following technique. It can clear that kind of STUFF out of you fast.

Wakeup Call

For you to succeed with the Wakeup Call technique, you'll need to position your awareness in the same direction you have been practicing with Be Deep and related techniques, paying quality attention with consciousness.

Read through the whole recipe first, then cook it!

1. Sit comfortably and close your eyes.
2. Be Deep: Notice what it is like to be you, right now. (No judging, please, just noticing.)
3. Open your eyes enough to read the following sequence of words. Say them out loud:

God, remove from my aura whatever does not belong to me.
Remove from my aura whatever does not belong to me.
Remove from my aura whatever does not belong to me.
Fill me with self-knowledge, self-love, spiritual light and spiritual power.

4. Be Deep: Notice what it is like to be you, right now. (Still no judging allowed! Simply notice whatever you happen to notice.)
5. End the experiment by saying something inside to end the technique, such as "Thank you" or "Experiment complete."
6. Open your eyes.

WHAT HAPPENED?

Whenever I teach Wakeup Call in workshops, most students report some immediate benefit, such as feeling:

- Clearer
- More awake inside
- Relaxed
- Calmer
- Less complicated, scattered or stressed out
- More like "me"

One technique — many possible results. So here's a smart move:

Expect nothing whatsover when you do this technique.

Of course, you didn't have this suggestion the first time. So when you were on your own, admit it. Were you trying to figure out what was supposed to happen and then make it happen? Were you hoping to feel a specific result?

From now on, trust yourself (and me) enough to be spontaneous, okay?

If you did the Wakeup Call innocently right from the start, congratulations. If not, try it again. Only this time, be willing to receive whatever you get.

Ironically, not trying for anything special is the best way to get results from any of the techniques in our 30-Day Plan. As a bonus, any results you do receive can then be valued as things that spontaneously happened, not things you were trying to make happen and, therefore, perfect for tying yourself up in knots of self-doubt.

Actually, some beginners must do the Wakeup Call several times before they notice much at all. Removing other people's STUFF from your aura causes subtle improvement.

These are not surface changes, such as you might notice from taking your banged-up car to the body shop.

So if you didn't notice much initially, don't be discouraged. Instead, resolve to be persistent.

Finally, keep in mind that you may have causes of STUFF other than what has been received from others through unskilled Empath

Merges. Don't expect this technique to heal STUFF that landed within you long before you met people like Lexi. Instead, seek expert help from people who have learned other skill sets, like cutting cords of attachment or healing astral-level debris.

Still you may be amazed how big a difference the Wakeup Call can make.

YOUR ASSIGNMENT FOR DAY 5

Your assignment for today is to use the Wakeup Call three more times. Find out what happens.

Day 6. The Big Analogy

Have you noticed a difference yet? Every day that you use the techniques and ideas from our 30-Day Plan, you're waking up more from inside. Keep waking up more and more until you are fully awake.

SLAP!

Tradition has it that Zen masters sometimes wake up their students by giving them a hit on the head. I'm trying to do something similar, though less painful, through the pages of this book.

Of course, your goal isn't some huge spiritual enlightenment necessarily, just waking up consciousness enough to realize that you can direct it wherever you like. By rights, that is mostly towards yourself... not God or your favorite hobby or whichever random person happens to be in the room along with you.

Learn to pay loving attention to yourself. That is the purpose of your experimenting with the Wakeup Call technique from yesterday. Something similar happens when you sprinkle Be Deep throughout your day. Brave Explorer, you're using the power of your consciousness to become a Skilled Empath.

The following chapters will continue your progress at becoming self-aware in the way that makes all the difference between being a Skilled Empath vs. an Unskilled Empath, someone who constantly picks up STUFF from other people and suffers accordingly.

Today's chapter is going to be a bit different. No new techniques. Instead, I want to give you something to think about. It's my favorite theory about why empaths suffer so much, and how this suffering is the flip side of something positive.

FROM DAY ONE

Why were you born as an empath? Was God playing a big game of "Nyah Nyah?" Was the point, "I made you this way on purpose, and My goal was to make you suffer"?

I don't think so. Instead, I will give you a very bold analogy. To potty training.

Wouldn't it be convenient if God could have designed humans just a bit differently regarding the human elimination system? How very much nicer would it be if someone like you didn't need to do #1 or #2 until you were, say, three years old.

Forget about diapers. One merry morning, when you are ready, Mom escorts you to the toilet. Then she shows you two new reasons to use it.

Some things, alas, are not possible, not even for God or your mother. The only way Life's Great Engineer could give you an elimination system was to have it installed and fully functioning right from Day 1.

Although this is not one of your proudest childhood stories, chances are that one of your very first acts after birth was to salute your proud mother, the doctor, etc., by sharing your own personal bodily fluids. Messy but absolutely necessary!

Rumor has it, you also demonstrated your vocal power by screaming, crying, etc. What else were you supposed to do with it, celebrate your arrival by singing the national anthem? Or maybe you weren't supposed to use your voice at all until ready to say "Please" and "Thank you"?

Wise though you may be as a soul, you weren't born knowing everything. And that includes productive ways to use your empath gift(s).

The gifts of an empath really have plenty in common with pooping. Except God didn't give empath circuits to everyone, any more than He decided to give everybody cute knees.

But if God *did* design you an empath, apparently the only way He could do it was to install circuits fully switched on right from birth. Think about it:

- Pooping isn't like talent for playing guitar, developed after you take some lessons.
- Pooping isn't like learning to drive a car, once you are old enough for a learner's permit.
- Pooping is a major, life-long ability, active right from the start.

In these ways, being born as an empath is exactly like being born able to poop. Your circuits are switched on right from birth.

TROUBLE IN EDEN

What if people had never learned to control their in-built poop circuits? Every-where you went, you'd hear the complaints.

Adam: Life is so messy.
Eve: I know just what you mean. That smell. It's awful.
Adam: Well, let's be good sports.
Eve: And don't forget the social skills, Honey. Never wave your used fig leaves in front of others. Hide them, so you can develop true dignity.

Luckily for us all, society has figured out skills for managing those poop circuits. Soon as you're old enough, you learn an excellent skill set called "Potty Training." This gives you control, so you don't keep the ON position going constantly.

Instead, you mostly keep those circuits turned OFF, saving up the impulse. Then, in a chosen place, at a chosen time, you will con-sciously choose to turn those circuits fully ON. And I'll bet you do a fine job of that, too.

Well, folks, that's very much like becoming a Skilled Empath. So if it cheers you, go forth and consider that Empath Empowerment is just a fancy term that means "Potty Training for Empaths."

Although you learned the toilet skills long ago, you may remem-ber that, back in the day, this type of learning involved paying atten-tion to yourself from inside.

Sure, there are social implications of being potty trained. Yet the skill doesn't come from having Aunt Myrtle follow you around for the rest of your life, asking every five minutes, "Dear, do you have to go to the big kid's room now?"

For both skill sets, the source of control lies within you. Rest assured, if you were coordinated enough to learn potty training, you're fully capable of becoming a Skilled Empath.

YOUR ASSIGNMENT FOR DAY 6

Think about this analogy, today. Not obsessively, and not just the potty part. Remember occasionally that you can use your own consciousness circuits to pay attention to yourself as The Most Important Person in the Room.

Just because someone else happens to be in the room to distract you, must you lose bladder control? Well, it's exactly the same with your empath circuits.

Paying attention to yourself as the main person — that can be easy. No need to sit in the midst of a party wearing a forced expression, until it's so obvious you're straining that Aunt Myrtle must grab you by the elbow, forcibly escorting you to that special room.

Be natural about this. A few times during the day, experiment with Be Deep and Wakeup Call. Pay attention to yourself in that quality way, Brave Explorer. Then you'll be ready to graduate to Part Two of Empath Empowerment.

Becoming a Skilled Empath

PART TWO:
Strengthen Your Way of Being You

What happens when you feel and act like The Most Important Person in the Room? The difference is symbolized in the picture opposite, where "You" are fully in focus while others fade into the background.

As The Most Important Person in The Room, you can still engage with others, and do it as someone who is compassionate, kind and thoughtful. But you can do this while keeping your empath gift(s) turned firmly OFF.

Must you keep living this way for the rest of your life? Of course not. After completing our 30-Day Plan — even during Part Three of this book — sometimes you will choose to turn your gift(s) ON.

In every case, however, that can be a choice. Quite a contrast to the habit of an unskilled empath, which is to keep each gift perpetually turned all the way ON!

Boldly break your old habit of doing unskilled Empath Merges. Instead, experiment with how you hold a space. Mostly pay attention to yourself — which is what healthy non-empaths always do.

Putting yourself first, you'll make subtle shifts that direct your consciousness. This is not the same thing as trying to manipulate your personality or social boundaries.

These subtle shifts of consciousness won't seem fake. They won't hurt anyone. Techniques that I share with you in Part Two will be for your private exploration.

Other folks won't disappear. Or be hurt. Or, probably, even notice.

Day 7. Body Day

"Stop taking on random STUFF from others." What, in practice, does that mean? You experiment with being The Most Important Person in the Room.

DIFFERENT FROM "BOUNDARIES"

As I introduce you to this new phase of your Empath Empowerment training, please note the context. We are NOT having a conversation about social behavior. Boundaries are NOT what we're exploring.

Boundaries involve behavior. Toddlers, for instance, have a strong sense of boundaries. Everything is "Mine."

We grownups are different because we learn manners. Sometimes we learn manners so well that, whether empaths or non-empaths, we forget our appropriate social boundaries.

Then we need Psychology Talk, such as:

- "No, you don't have to give your nice coat away, just because someone else admires it."
- "If you've been mixing up your needs with the needs of other people, stop."

Good advice to be sure! Nonetheless, social-level advice is irrelevant to our skill set. This 30-Day Plan involves waking up consciousness from inside yourself.

Mastering this, learning many approaches and developing finesse with your own consciousness — this will help you to form new habits about how you treat yourself. Changes to social behavior, if needed, will develop automatically. Do first things first.

Empaths have a tendency to identify strongly with being other people. Hannah's back pain becomes your pain. Lexi's longing for friendship becomes your longing. And you already know how much fun *that* is!

When you become The Most Important Person in the Room, what doesn't happen? Being in the room with other people, you don't automatically drift into identifying with them. One way to break that habit is to make today (and part of every day) Body Day.

The Pinch of Life

Imagine, you've drifted off to sleep. Or maybe not. Hmm, you're not sure.

What's a quick 'n easy way to tell? Pinch yourself.

Hey, I can't take credit for inventing this technique, but it's still a good one for our skill set.

If awake, one pinch will give you the familiar and unmistakable sensation of being in your physical body. If dreaming, a pinch can't duplicate that sensation.

I call it "The Pinch of Life," as in "Human Life When Wide Awake" and "Life in My Physical Body."

Give yourself a pinch if you start drifting into the experience of being another person in the room.

Say that you're with Troy, star forward among the neighborhood soccer guys, a person of immense prestige and fascination. He's describing his latest triumph doing a hat trick, and you're just enthralled, listening and (without trying to, consciously) supporting him with your auric energy.

Eventually, you will have a moment of choice. This will be subtle, not like hearing a referee blow a whistle and scream "Red card." Instead, you'll realize something like:

"I'm getting so involved in listening to Troy. Maybe it's time to go back to making MYSELF The Most Important Person in The Room."

Give yourself a quick pinch, on the hand or somewhere else inconspicuous.

> *Hello! I'm alive in my own body and I know it!*
> Usually, that's all it takes for you to resume your rightful place
> as The Most Important Person in The Room. If not, add the
> Be Deep Quickie.

Here comes the really wild part. After you do The Pinch, will Troy notice the difference? Probably not. Assuming that he's a non-empath, he's used to feeling like The Most Important Person in The Room. Troy will do just fine. While you will get to feel like YOU.

Whenever you realize that you have a choice about being The Most Important Person in The Room, wake yourself up, even if you have to use a little pinch to do so.

Notice, you never need ask permission before shifting attention back to yourself. Moving your consciousness is not like elementary school, where you had to raise your hand for approval before you could go to the water fountain. Move your consciousness freely whenever you like.

GOT A PROBLEM WITH THAT?

Sometimes empaths fear that if they withdraw the support of their consciousness, other people will crumble like a harshly treated saltine. If you're worrying, answer these questions.

1. Will other people really die without having me as their version of life support?
2. Then how *do* they manage without me when I'm not in the room with them?
3. Might they also have been created with an inner consciousness?
4. Might each person, not only me, possess a vital link to God that can be used as a source of supply?
5. Did God make all other people super-fragile, while I am the only strong one?
6. Is there really any grown-up on earth who depends on being nurtured by my consciousness and personal energy?
7. Why?

The problem comes down to *enabling*. That means protecting someone, like an alcoholic, from the consequences of his/her own problems. By enabling, you help that person short-term, but long-term you're keeping him/her stuck in a limiting pattern.

Let's assume that Troy is so energetically feeble that he must cling to others energetically. Where is it written that the person depended upon must be YOU?

If you stop volunteering to supplying your energy, can't the Troy's of the world still find a way to survive? (Hint: What, you think you're the only empath on earth?)

Cool Extras

During Body Day, it's helpful to have many ways to wake up your physical awareness. Here are other techniques that I like. Or create techniques of your own.

• Feel your heartbeat or touch the pulse on your wrist. Is it slow and steady? Scared and rabbit-like? Explore.

• Find the nearest mirror. Take a look at yourself. Even if other people nearby are reflected there, you can find yourself, right? It's a good objective reminder that you ARE in the room in the first place. This will make it easier to consider yourself The Most Important Person in The Room.

• Rub two fingers together, like thumb and forefinger. Doing this very discretely can remind you, "Hey, I'm here."

• Even more secretly, wiggle your toes.

YOUR ASSIGNMENT FOR DAY 7

Celebrate your body today, Brave Explorer, by paying it some positive attention. Do this however and wherever you like. How often will you choose to pay attention to your physical self? That's nobody else's business.

Body Day is a vital part of your skill set for Empath Empowerment. Still, it is just one part. So, please, if someone demands that you explain your 30-Day Plan in 30 seconds, for pity's sake, don't say, "All you have to do is wiggle your toes."

Day 8. Mind Day

Paying attention to yourself yesterday, rather than the Troy's and Lexi's of the world, did you notice? Nobody died.

Empaths tend to support others constantly with awareness. You may not realize you're doing this until you stop for a while. Then you get it.

Now let's help you get it even better.

Empath's Pantomime

Other people probably need way less support than you have been giving them. Here's a way to prove this to yourself. It's a pair exercise I developed for a workshop.

For this version you will need a partner, but this other person doesn't have to be an empath, merely somebody who is both alive, human and willing to play a silly game with you.

When you're going to do the exercise and not just read about it, find that volunteer. Stand opposite each other.

You'll be taking turns, Brave Explorer. First time around, one of you plays The Leader. The other will act as The Follower. Second time around, switch. Here's what to do.

1. For two minutes, The Leader moves slowly into different positions, changing the angles of arms, legs, head, etc.
2. The Follower's job is to copy the Leader's motions, like a pantomime artist.
3. After you're done, discuss what this exercise was like for you in both roles, being The Leader and also being The Follower.

PROBLEM SOLVING

Reflecting on your experiences with Empath's Pantomime, could you possibly have been doing more than I asked?

When you were *The Follower*, were you inwardly trying to make things nice for The Leader? Remember, your job was just to copy The Leader's movements. Besides that, were you sending out a supportive kind of energy? For instance, you could have been giving nonverbal cues like "I'm ready now for your next move"?

When you were *The Leader*, were you trying to make things nice for The Follower? That might include making sure the tempo was suitable, not doing anything too challenging, etc. Instead of focusing mostly on leading during this exercise, did you focus at least as much on helping your partner do the job of following you?

The first time I assigned this exercise in a workshop, I asked my Pantomime Artists if this had been the case. Some got it right away and started to laugh. Others skeptically said, "Noooooooooooooooooooo."

So I told them, "Prove it." The whole group was instructed to repeat the exercise, only this time to keep it simple. "If you lead, just lead. If you follow, just follow. Later, we'll discuss your experiences."

Were those skeptics ever surprised! Doing their second round of Empath's Pantomime, they realized they *had* been doing a lot with their consciousness, far more than they meant to. Why? Supportive volunteer work had been an unquestioned habit.

A habit?

Yes, a habit.

That habit of supporting others with your consciousness is the habit we're going to change, starting now. This silly habit corresponds to merging your aura with people for no good reason, except that they happen to be in the room with you.

Focus on yourself from now on, okay? Keep things simple. You could even call it "Keep things surface."

And if you have a partner nearby, do a second round of Empath's Pantomime, focusing just on yourself, The Most Important Person in the Room.

CELEBRATE MIND DAY

Taking self-awareness further, let's consider what it means to *use your mind*. This contrasts to what most empaths do on a daily basis, which is *lose your mind*. Why lose your mind? Because you're so busy paying attention to everyone else.

What is your mind, anyway? By definition (and meaning no insult) your mind is surprisingly simple. Not simple-minded, just human.

NO TRAFFIC ACCIDENTS FOR 2,000,000 MILES

Deb Davis is a long haul truck driver for Frito-Lay. After 26 years, she won an award from the company for driving two million miles without an accident. Deb lives in Wisconsin, which gets its share of snow. But she's never had a traffic accident at work. Neither has she ever had a car crash.

What is the secret of Deb's perfect driving record? She was asked this during an interview on the National Public Radio show "All Things Considered."

Deb's answer? "Paying attention."

Driving is "very, very simple," according to Deb Davis. She explained that if she ever got in an accident it would mean that she wasn't doing what she was supposed to be doing as a driver, paying attention.

According to Ms. Davis, life is very simple if you let it be.

What makes this award-winning driver so special? Maybe it's just that she uses her mind.

To be human means that you have both a simple mind and a complicated intellect. Tomorrow will be Intellect Day. Today is Mind Day, where you get to explore the glories of your mind and how that trusty mind of yours can help with Empath Empowerment. ·

What's the difference between mind and intellect? Telling the difference can seem tricky at first because both mind and intellect function by means of thoughts. But with the mind, thoughts employ concepts you've already mastered. For instance:

- Point to 10 different things in the place where you are right now, counting out loud as you go.
- Name 10 different colors in the place where you are right now, naming each color out loud.

- Which are you doing right now, swimming or reading? You can't be doing both. Because you are human, your mind allows you to do just one thing, at a time.

For humans, using your mind is a way to do only one thing at a time, and do it with single focus: Chop wood. Carry water. Drink the water. Don't try drinking the wood.

If you were God, your mind might work differently. But, with all respect, when was the last time anyone called you omniscient? Being human, whenever you wish, you can favor this simple-minded version of reality called "the mind." To wake up your mind, list out loud whatever you're doing, one thing at a time, one thought at a time.

Mindfulness can be very soothing. It can create a kind of mini-eternity, only set in the present. When you are being mindful, it's impossible to rush. As one of my students put it, "All the busy-ness goes away when I enter the practical Mind."

WHO'S IN CHARGE OF YOUR MIND?

It's you, of course. You're in charge even if another person happens to be in the room with you. You're in charge even if you used to have the habit of treating that other person like The Most Important Person in the Room.

Habits or no habits, you haven't relinquished control. Potentially at least, you are always in control of your mind. To stay in control, make one simple choice here and now. Choose where to direct your attention.

For example, let's say that you speak English but you have also managed to learned another language. Say it's Swahili. Great!

Now, imagne that you're walking down the street, talking with a friend, and busily thinking away in English. Does it ever happen that Swahili randomly takes you over and suddenly, it's got to be all Swahili, all the time?

Nope. Assuming that you are sane, you get to choose. Speaking an extra language doesn't mean switching tongues for no reason. You're the one in control of your languages. And you're also in control of your mind. Which brings us to your assignment for today, Brave Explorer.

Sharpen Your Mind

There's a story I want you to tell yourself. It's the story of your life, as experienced with your mind.

Nothing intimidating here. Just supply a short play-by-play commentary for a minute, out loud. Observe the surface facts, just the facts. Automatically, this will to shift attention to your mind. For example:

I'm in the room with Roscoe. I hear him speak Swahili. I'm sitting on the sofa. As I look around, I notice that this room has additional furniture, and it also has a floor and a ceiling. Now I hear the sound of clinking. It comes from the ice cubes in my glass of soda. I am holding this glass. I am holding up to my lips. I raise the upper lip and tilt the glass. Liquid transfers from the glass into my body. There is a taste of Coca-Cola.

Nothing fancy here, right? Yet telling this mind-level story is balm to your mind.

Whenever you speak your surface story out loud, that positions your consciousness firmly in that inner category called "Mind."

Thinking that story will do the same thing, as long as you're not multi-tasking. (Multi-tasking automatically brings awareness to the intellect.)

For this technique, I'm recommending that you do the narration out loud to help you become totally focused and clear, sharpening your mind.

Choosing to be mindful, for your sole benefit, helps you to become The Most Important Person in The Room. It's one more way to turn your empath's gift(s) OFF.

"Golly," you may be thinking. "An awful lot of people today must have very sharp minds because they're constantly talking drivel like 'I am here. I am standing outside. I am calling you and it is two o'clock.'"

Yes, people are saying the obvious, often saying it very loudly, on their cells. Or they're twittering. Or they're social networking. Much of the vital news report sounds just like this.

However, that isn't the same thing as Sharpen Your Mind, which is being used as a technique to wake up the mind. This exercise is to be done privately.

Mindfulness techniques are not generally done as a form of communication, nor are they used for "parallel play" (a term coined by experts at early childhood development).

Using technology to broadcast experiences of personal mindfulness, such as twittering, will not increase self-awareness. Instead, this is a great example of communication that is wide rather than personal, shallow rather than deep.

The thrill of these fads includes using a new medium to reach out and touch as many people as possible, empath or non-empath, strangers or friends, into you or not really

Whatever the content of such communications, they belong to the category of the environment, not mind, body. spirit, intellect, soul, or emotions. Each of these categories will be explored during our 30-Day Plan.

In our Plan there is no Twitter Day. But there is definitely Mind Day. And it is now.

YOUR ASSIGNMENT FOR DAY 8

Do Sharpen Your Mind for one minute. Automatically, you'll direct your consciousness to that category of experience.

For heaven's sake, don't spend this entire day doing this. Used sparingly, Sharpen Your Mind can be powerful stuff. Sprinkle just a little throughout today.

Use the technique maybe that three or four random times during your day, tops. (Unless, like Deb Davis, you're driving a huge truck filled with corn chips and other snack foods.)

As always, remember to use your Wakeup Technique any time you suspect that you have been taking on other people's STUFF.

Simple, natural shifts of consciousness, or a quick affirmation out loud — this won't win you record numbers of text messages. But it sure can help you to become a Skilled Empath... who happens to be The Most Important Person in the Room.

Day 9. Intellect Day

Q. *Enough already. I've paid enough attention to myself. It feels different, all right. It feels selfish. Am I your first student to have this reaction?*
A. No, it's pretty common during the process of gaining Empath Empowerment. Paying so much attention to yourself, all kinds of doubts can arise.

Your intellect is dominating now, or you wouldn't be circling around with self-doubt. Let's emphasize your intellect's strengths, since it's so active.

Intellect is the category of yourself that you depend upon to evaluate things like "when have I done enough?" Intellect drives decision-making. Creativity, too.

Yesterday, Mind Day, you had ample opportunity to make yourself The Most Important Person in the Room by enjoying simple pleasures, like naming different colors around you.

Choosing not to let your consciousness slide into identifying with other people, you used your mind to gently bring attention back to yourself in present surroundings.

If your mind were a game, it would be *Bingo* or *lotto*. By contrast, your intellect (today's focus for exploration) is more like *scrabble* or *chess*. Your intellect is also required for that wildly popular postmodern game called "*multi-tasking.*"

Q. *Ha! I can prove you wrong. Say that my multitasking involves listening to music and eating my lunch. Why would my intellect be involved at all?*
A. Your intellect plays the role of traffic director. When your hand goes to turn up the volume of that music, it doesn't reach for your

mouth. Nor do you squish a spoonful of mashed potatoes into your sound equipment. (I'm hoping.)

Even if you are loving the food, and you only play music in the background for setting a mood to enhance the meal, what has been kissed goodbye? It's full awareness of your physical body.

Because you are playing that music, what has been put in charge? It's your intellect, which now must switch back and forth between the food and the music, maybe your emotions as well, deciding which category to favor when.

Q. Okay, then. But I already know what you're going to assign us for today. It's going to be like yesterday, only using the intellect. Boring!

Besides, what would make that different, really different, from spending my day doing some psychological exercise about protecting my boundaries?

A. Such a good question! It deserves a good-sized answer, even its very own heading....

RESISTANCE

For mastery at turning your empath gift(s) OFF, you must be able to direct your consciousness toward every category of your human equipment. Admittedly, you'll use only one category at a time. But it's best to keep every category available.

There are, after all, only seven: Mind, body, spirit, intellect, soul, emotions and environment.

By hook or by crook or by taking a look, you are developing skill with them all. Flexibility for shifting awareness is vital for Empath Empowerment. So is freedom. A special kind of freedom is yours when can you experience life through every one of these seven categories.

During this second part of our 30-Day Plan, yes, you're opening up the fullest awareness possible of each category. There's no substitute, not if you aim to develop a complete set of skills as an empath.

To become just a *semi-skilled empath*, you could get by with three or four categories. Yet wouldn't you prefer to develop the full skill set? Especially because, in doing so, you will become more self-actualized as a person!

For that, you'll need to learn how to activate awareness at *every* single category available to you as a human being, the entire set of seven. What's to keep you from doing that? Resistance. It can come up any day during our 30-Day Plan.

Should you feel resistance, consider the context. What was happening right before you started to feel that resistance?

Sometimes the very idea of playing with one category of your human self becomes a huge turn-off. Resistance will bring you feelings like "I don't wanna."

Actually, resistance can come in a thousand variations. For example, my questioner in today's chapter expressed resistance to paying attention to herself and then to using her intellect. It was Meg, actually. And if only you could have heard her tone of voice while asking these questions!

Normally Meg seems meek as could be. Just between you and me, this time her attitude really shocked me. She sounded arrogant and defensive.

That's fine with me, so long as she doesn't quit but follows our 30-Day Plan all the way through.

How about you? Have encountered resistance yet, during Body Day or Mind Day or any other part of our 30-Day Plan? Let's do some problem solving. What can you do if you start feeling that you just hate exploring some part of your human identity, such as your intellect?

Four choices are listed below. The first two could be called "bad," but they're also "popular" and "very human." The last two choices will serve you much better, especially in the long run.

1. BLAME

Should any aspect of yourself make you feel bored, trivialized, empty, sad, scared, etc., you might want to try blaming.

Rant about life or your childhood or how I'm teaching you through this book. Although blame doesn't really fix problems, it can be fun… and make you feel superior to whomever you blame.

2. ESCAPE

Whenever you encounter a dead spot within your own psyche, surely you can find ways to distract yourself. If you don't like using your mind, body, intellect, etc., don't. Instead, live in your feelings or spirituality all the time.

Many people do. And they're considered perfectly sane. (Marginally sane, anyway. Self-actualizing, no.)

Escaping can seem like the simplest possible solution. But it reminds me of Ethel, a woman I knew in college who didn't like vegetables. At age 20, she decided that henceforth she would never eat a vegetable again.

Problem solved. In a way.

You could have a pretty good life despite hating and ignoring categories of yourself, but I guarantee you'll have a better life by making your peace with them.

3. LOVE YOUR PROBLEM TO DEATH

Let's say that you don't enjoy doing one of the techniques from our 30-Day Plan. Instead of escape or blaming, you could go back and do that technique again and again. Continue until you stop resisting it.

For instance, say that you hated doing the exercise to "Sharpen Your Mind." In this case, out of self-love (not masochism) you could repeat Mind Day. You could stretch your personal growth even further by doing Mind Week.

Meaning what? Every day for that week, you would keep on playing with mindfulness a few times daily, undeterred by resistance.

Any time your own mind seems scary, you can give that resistance a big, loud "Ha, ha, ha." Then you return to the same technique, just for a minute or so. Then consider yourself wildly successful, both at practicing the technique and at melting resistance.

Yes, a relentless approach like this can melt resistance away. Only be sure to treat yourself lovingly, not harshly. Soon, you'll become a person who likes your own mind or body or whatever.

4. SEEK PROFESSIONAL HELP

Once upon a time, some of my students had pretty severe problems with resistance to experiencing to their own minds, emotions, etc. They weren't crazy, just what psychologists call "the worried well."

Some chose to do healing sessions with me, where I helped them move STUFF out of their auras by cutting cords of attachment, etc. Afterwards they moved forward much faster at Empath Empowerment.

If you find yourself battling any aspect of yourself, you might want to seek help from a healer who seems compatible. Professional services can save enormous amounts of time and frustration, so don't be cheap with yourself.

Do-it-yourself efforts work only up to a point. A professional could save you years of struggle against resistance. In fact, you might need just a session or two with a regression therapist, specialist at Emotional Freedom Technique, etc.

WAKE UP YOUR INTELLECT

Now that we have dealt with resistance (in theory, at least) let's prepare for Intellect Day. Here are four different techniques to wake up your intellect. All are to be used in your personal life only, not while you're at work.

To liven up each technique, I'll supply examples by bringing in various buddies from our Cast of Characters.

Depth Probe

This is a technique to use while you're interacting with someone else, especially being together in the same room.

Use your intellect to define how deeply you need to be involved in the relationship.

While you're with James, for instance, take a few seconds (only) to think about questions like these:

+ "What is James really saying here? Is there a subtext that I'm noticing to the point where I ignore his actual words?"
+ "Is James asking me to help him in any way or is he simply talking?"
+ "What is in it for me right now, hanging out with James?"

Whatever answer you receive, accept it. Then return to engaging fully in your conversation.

The point of this silent inquiry is simply to switch on your intellect.

Might you learn something from the Depth Probe that causes you to make changes in how you relate to your friend?

Sure, but that's optional, just an extra benefit of doing the technique. Even if you don't change a thing about how you interact with James, just by doing the Depth Probe, you win. Victory means this: You have used your intellect to wake up from inside.

Victory or not, easy does it. Depth Probe is best used for only a few seconds at a time. You question. You answer. Then return to the conversation.

Only a few seconds — that's very important. The goal of Empath Empowerment is a natural state of being The Most Important Person in The Room. This differs from detaching intellectually throughout an entire conversation.

DETACHMENT

Hannah, from our Cast of Characters, detaches from conversations constantly. She's been detaching for years in a misguided attempt to shut out the pain from others, trying to do what we'd call "becoming a Skilled Empath." It's a technique she figured out for herself, so she's very proud of it.

If you've ever talked with someone like Hannah, you know her detachment fools nobody, at least nobody who is a Highly Sensitive Person, which means 1 in 5 human beings.

On the receiving end of Hannah's detachment, you know how artificial — even manipulative — her behavior appears. Ironically, it doesn't even work for the purpose intended.

Hannah's method is to use detachment to stop picking up other people's pain and maintain a strong, healthy sense of self. Unfortunately, it never improves a person's quality of life to overuse one category.

A week has seven days, not just Mondays. A rainbow has seven colors, not only yellow. And a human being has seven inner modes, or categories, not only intellect but mind-body-spirit-soul-emotions-environment.

No one category of human potential (in Hannah's case, her intellect) can stop her from doing unskilled Empath Merges. So STUFF slips into Hannah's aura even while she valiantly uses her intellect to distance herself from others.

At best, Hannah's overuse of the intellect represents a brave attempt, a gimmick, a kind of busy work.

You can do so much better. So I'm warning you. Depth Probe for minutes is a fabulously helpful technique for Empath Empowerment. But if you use it for hours, rather than minutes, you risk becoming detached, like Hannah. Use any technique like Depth Probe very sparingly.

A second technique for Intellect Day doesn't bring on detachment but, instead, amps up your natural curiosity.

YOUR FIRST LOYALTY

Before learning our next technique, here come some questions. When you're with other adults, is your first loyalty to them or to yourself?

If they asked you to donate an arm, you might not think twice. But what if you were asked to give them major chunks of your consciousness?

In fact, what if you have been volunteering to do this in ways that haven't been necessary?

Hey, as The Most Important Person in the Room, you can habitually put yourself first, and do it without appearing grotesquely conceited.

Say that you're in a room with James and the rest of the cocktail party. Are you really enjoying your conversation with him? If not, remember this saying: *So many men, so little time!*

While with him, you can allow your head to swivel occasionally, noticing other available people... or anything else in the room that you might wish to notice instead of that likeable but sleep-inducing James.

Unless you're nailed to the floor, you do have freedom of movement, correct?

If you're stuck there chatting with James, not enjoying yourself, you probably don't need to wait until HE says goodbye.

How often have you passively waited for another person to end a conversation? Is the purpose of relationships really to be of service to others until they have sucked you dry?

Yet sometimes it isn't socially appropriate to do a head swivel, followed by a heel swivel, and say goodbye to well meaning James. When you're stuck, use Cocktail Party.

In this technique, your intellect helps you to question reality, very helpful if you must stay put. I call it "Cocktail Party" because these light-hearted social events are famous for fickleness. Heads swivel freely. Once a conversation turns even slightly boring, suave cocktail party guests will offer a flimsy excuse and scamper away. You can do a version of this while staying put.

Cocktail Party

That's how it's done, Dahling. These events don't have to be taken seriously. You're not consulting with the Delphic Oracle. It's only a silly cocktail party.

During your conversation with James, at any random time, remember your inner freedom of movement. So often, an empath doesn't play anything remotely resembling "Cocktail Party."

Before today, if you literally were at a cocktail party, would you scamper away when bored? Heavens no. You were more likely to act as though locked in a confessional — on the priest's side — possibly stuck there for hours.

Our Cocktail Party technique gives you permission to scamper more and suffer less and never worry that exercising freedom of choice makes you "bad."

Move away inwardly, that's all. Pay only enough attention to James so that you can nod your head appropriately when he pauses his monologue. Otherwise indulge in your own thoughts, feelings, physical sensations, etc. Let your intellect act as "The Switcher."

Our next technique won't necessarily cause inner swiveling. But inwardly you could start doing a Snoopy dance.

Insisting

In the midst of talking to strangers or friends, you do have the right to enjoy yourself. Insist on it. Let's say you're talking with Roscoe.

+ When in doubt about having fun, use your intellect to pose this very useful question: "Am I having fun right now?"
+ If you're enjoying Roscoe' company, go with the flow.
+ If you're not having fun, and it's socially acceptable to leave, end the conversation and leave.
+ What if you're not having a great time but duty requires that you stay there with Roscoe? You can still find a way to have fun. Use your intellect as a tool for secret enjoyment.

Intellect can be great for that. Your intellect offers countless ways to slice, dice or chop your reality, helping you to notice whatever you find interesting.

Yes, you're allowed to secretly use that intellect wherever you happen to be. When you insist on enjoying yourself, your intellect can help make it happen.

I remember reading an interview with Jodie Foster, a brilliant woman, a Yale grad and, also, an actress since childhood. Jodie has spent long periods of time hanging around movie sets. So the interviewer asked how she coped with being bored on the set.

How did Jodie answer? "I've never been bored in my life."

Now, there's a person who knows how to use her intellect. Sound like you to you? If not, you can become that kind of person.

What happens when you insists on having fun? It works because you have every right to do that. Use your intellect, or any other compartment of yourself, to enjoy your life. Pay attention to anything you like, such as:

- Silently do Face Reading on others in the room
- Listen to the quality of voices, the underlying silence, whatever sounds are within earshot
- Find your favorite colors in the room. Enjoy how they look
- Compare and contrast the shapes of nearby objects as though you were an artist
- Ask questions that would make the conversation become more interesting

Yes, you can do your duty but still find a way to have fun. And that's one way to understand what it means, being The Most Important Person in The Room.

Transferable Email Skill

Just because you've got mail, must you scrutinize every message word for word? That way, you'd never leave your computer. *You* might start to feel like spam, you'd be reading so much of it.

Surely you have developed survival skills for dealing with spam. Even genuine emails where your friend Jocelyn describes her latest pedicure in thrilling detail! Just because messages fill up your in-box doesn't mean that you are required to read every word.

If Zachary happens to be in the room with you, rather than your in-box, you're still in charge of message management.

Should Zachary seem annoyingly intense, or unbelievably boring, you can treat him like spam. Inwardly press "delete."

In human terms, what does it mean to stay in a social situation after you press "delete"? Brave Explorer, you're allowed to just go through the motions.

When someone sends you an email that you don't like for any reason, you know how to treat that email. Just because someone stands before you in 3-D, why should that inner power diminish?

How appropriate that Intellect Day would be packed with new techniques! Any one of them can help you relish your discerning, delightful, direct-able intellect.

Do remember, Brave Explorer, that today's adventures are only part of Empath Empowerment, not the whole thing.

It can be tempting to confuse intellectual games with changing reality beyond the intellect. Ideally, you'll use today's four techniques as just part of your 30-Day Plan for Empath Empowerment. Don't stop here.

YOUR ASSIGNMENT FOR DAY 9

Today's assignment is to use your intellect as a means to make yourself The Most Important Person in the Room. As with previous days, I'm not suggesting that you go into a long-term detached state. Simply use your intellect as a trigger to emphasize your personal experience.

Choose from our four techniques for today or make up new techniques to switch on your intellect.

Supplementing this, you also can do the Wakeup Call any time it's needed. (That's getting to be a habit, right?)

Day 10. Emotions Day

Saddle up, cowboys and cowgirls. You have a big herd to tend today. Those "cattle" are your emotions.

Notice them grazing free over the plains: Large cows, little calves, and the occasional frolicsome bull. Each one is named after an emotion, like *Humperdinck the Melancholy*. And they're all yours.

So herd those cows today, because emotions are another self-category that a Skilled Empath needs to know well from the inside.

Am I suggesting that you spend all day contemplating your astrological chart, your navel or that large spotted animal down yonder named *Bessie, Who Languishes Due to Frustrated Rebelliousness?*

Heck, no. You're just doing the same basic moves as you did on Body Day, Mind Day or Intellect Day. Gently you're paying occasional attention to this chosen category of your mind-body-spirit-intellect-soul-emotions-environment.

Quick Emotional Healing

Ah, emotions. My emotions!
If ever you find yourself caught up in emotions belonging to others — their problems, their thinking, their religious conflicts, their fears about the environment; emotions of any kind, even mild jealousy over "Ooh, Zachary's fantastic hairstyle" — what can you do about it?

1. Start with a round of Be Deep. You are you, not anyone else.
2. Soon as possible, use your Wakeup Call to clear out your aura. (Really, it's no bigger a deal than blowing your nose.

> Only you'll use a few well chosen words rather than tis-
> sues.)
> 3. Immediately afterwards, pay attention to your emotions for
>   a few seconds.

Whenever you find yourself straying into other people's inner experiences, instead of your own, *Whoa buckaroo, don't you have some herd-
ing to do?*

HERDING AND BRANDING

Personally, I think that branding an animal is disgusting. Imagine having a searing hot iron pushed into *your* flesh, just so you can proudly
wear the name of some ranch, like "The Lazy Overachiever."

However we're doing a mere thought experiment. Our "brand"
won't be a hot piece of metal, more like a slogan. And using it should
never produce a smell like some panicked, burning, sweaty animal.

Really, it can be quite simple to claim your own emotions and
find them more interesting than emotions belonging to other people.
Just use our next technique.

Brand Your Cattle

This technique is designed to help you distinguish your emotions from the emotions of others.
Say the following set of affirmations out loud. (If it would be
socially awkward to speak the affirmations out loud, your second best choice would be to simply think the words.)

Right here and now, I choose to turn my empath gift(s) OFF.
For now, my emotions are the only ones I feel deeply.
If I notice emotions belonging to others, it is safe for me to
pay attention just on the surface.
It is easy for me to be in touch with my human emotions.
For now, I pay attention at depth to my emotions only.

> For the next minute, pay close attention to your emotions in the here and now, whatever those emotions happen to be.
> Please notice that technical term "next minute." This does not mean "forever" or even "for the rest of my day."
> Do this technique for a short time only. Then go back to being "a normal person" (whatever that is for you).

That final point is important. For Emotions Day, you don't have to use the "Brand Your Cattle" technique constantly. Please do not think that you have just received a set of magical affirmations, so all you need do is repeat these words all day and you will automatically become a Skilled Empath.

The "Brand Your Cattle" technique is one part of your skill set for Empath Empowerment. If you have the gift of Emotional Intuition or Emotional Oneness (or both), Brand Your Cattle could become an especially important skill. But it's helpful for all empaths, regardless of which gift(s) you have.

Use this technique whenever you want to point your consciousness away from other people's emotions and back in the direction that makes you The Most Important Person in The Room.

Not only can this technique become a useful part of Emotions Day. So can the general idea of *paying attention at depth to your emotions only.* Does that mean you will never enjoy that interesting experience of doing a Skilled Empath Merge? Of course not.

As a Skilled Empath, sometimes you will choose to turn your gift(s) ON. We will get to that later in our 30-Day Plan. Promise! Meanwhile, I don't want to alarm you but, for most of my students, a healthy ratio of Empath OFF to Empath ON is about 28:2.

That's right, as a graduate of our 30-Day Plan, you'll average spending 28 minutes on yourself before lavishing 2 minutes on somebody else, doing a Skilled Empath Merge or the equivalent.

Coincidentally that ratio of 28 OFF to 2 ON is exactly what we have in this book.

Is that fair? Sure — fair to you, Brave Explorer. To be effective at helping others, as well as effective at maintaining your sanity, empaths need to turn their gift(s) firmly OFF most of the time. Surely I don't have to remind you of our lovely analogy about potty training....

NAME THOSE CUTE LITTLE COWS

What will happen today as you turn ON deep awareness of your emotions and turn OFF deep emotional awareness of other people?

Regarding other people, a better way to make contact with their feelings is to use "Emotional Intelligence."

This useful concept was developed by Daniel Goleman, Ph.D., author of a bestselling book called *Emotional Intelligence.* The brilliant Dr. Goleman, and his aura, are living proof that a person can develop superb skill at Emotional Intelligence without being an empath.

To simply Goleman's important discovery, Emotional Intelligence requires that you name emotions belonging to others as well as yourself, then get a sense of social politics between people and act appropriately to fit in. Emotions show in tone of voice, facial expression, body language, as well as the actual words being spoken out loud.

Anyone can learn Emotional Intelligence. It's actually a way to use your mind (i.e., having thoughts about emotions). For instance, let's take another look at our Cast of Characters near the front of this book, Page x. I'll name the emotions I think they're having. Right now:

- Troy is happy.
- James is depressed.
- Lexi is secretly smug.
- Roscoe is grumpy but hiding it well.

Figure out emotional labels like these in real life situations and you win the prize every time. Meanwhile, back at the ranch, you can name all *your* cute little cows.

Emotional Intelligence for an Empath

Here's how to use Emotional Intelligence on Emotions Day — and whenever else you wish to turn off unskilled Empath Merges.

Remember that feeling other people's feelings is optional. Often you can substitute Emotional Intelligence.

As a born empath, you're fully capable of doing a Skilled Empath Merge, as appropriate (Once you've learned how. We'll get there!) But that's powerful, not something to do casually whenever another human being crosses your path.

In most cases, you'll choose NOT to do an Empath Merge. What then?

Rather than feeling other people's emotions directly, you can merely recognize them. Seal the deal by *naming* the different emotions inwardly.

This enables you to make contact with emotions in a way that will show in your face, voice and behavior. So you can act appropriately, even be more helpful than otherwise.

Yet you will be spared from emotionally roller coastering your way through a conversation.

Feeling other people's feelings along with them — why do that? Having a simple conversation, you're not obligated to do a simultaneous translation into Greek, either.

Don't be scared of this technique, Brave Explorer. Try it for just today. And supplement it, too. It can also be helpful to use Emotional Intelligence on yourself occasionally.

Locating your emotions doesn't just help you make sense of your inner life. Staying in touch with your feelings on a regular basis can make an empath less likely to project feelings onto others. You'll also find it easier to keep your empath gift(s) turned OFF.

Some of you empaths already find it super easy to notice your own emotions. But some of you may find it difficult. You may even discover, to your horror, that you seem to have no emotions whatsoever. Our next technique can help.

Emotional GPS

Being human, at any given time, you always have at least one emotion. And you were born with a Global Positioning System for finding words to express it. To locate a name for whatever you're feeling, right here and now:

1. Close your eyes.
2. Take a deep breath.

3. Notice which emotion(s) you have.

4. Ask inside for words for your feelings. Emotions have names, and you know those names. Ask. This will help you make contact with the appropriate name, no effort needed.

5. Optional: If you feel the least bit stuck, don't concentrate or struggle. Take a few slow, deep breaths; then repeat Steps 3-4.

6. Open your eyes just long enough to write down whatever names you get.

7. Inside, say something like, "Good job! And now this technique is done."

8. Open your eyes.

Look over what you wrote. Sometimes it is easy to name your emotions. It can be fun.

However, some of you Brave Explorers may not notice any emotions at all. Or you may even call some experiences emotions when they really are something else.

Then it's time to do some problem solving. Don't let any problems discourage you, because you definitely have what it takes to find and name your emotions.

For decades, I have worked with clients and students. Often I have asked them to tell me what they are feeling emotionally. Most of them don't do this very well, not at first. But after a little problem solving, they find it easy to name their emotions. That's why I'm so sure all of you can do that, too.

Let's do problem solving now in the form of Q&A conversations with empaths who find it hard to name their emotions.

None of the following questioners has made contact with an emotion and named it. Yet they're oh-so-close.

Mostly problems arise when people don't aim their consciousness in the right direction for finding an emotion. Soon as you read each question, can you spot what's wrong?

Q. Meg: In my childhood I used to have the most wonderful time making a wish upon a star. That's an emotion, isn't it?

A. That's an idea from your intellect, an idea about an emotion — which is not the same thing as an actual emotion.

What shows that your words have come from your intellect? You were describing a memory, not an experience in the here and now.

Intellect is fine, and you certainly don't have to destroy your intellect to be able to make contact with your emotions. Your goal is to to use all the different categories within yourself: Mind, body, spirit, intellect, soul, emotions, environment.

Only the goal is also to use each category for what it does best, not as a substitute for another type of inner perception.

Most of these categories work only in present time: Emotions, mind, body, soul and environment. Only intellect and spirit can move a person through space and time.

"In my childhood I used to" is, therefore, a tipoff that you have shifed to intellect. Intellect Day is not today!

No worries, Meg. Close your eyes. Go inside and explore the feeling connected to *"I used to have the most wonderful time making a wish upon a star."*

Poke around. You're sure to find at least one emotion. It might be:

- Wistful
- Nostalgic
- Tragic
- Hopeful

Feel it. And then you can name it. Score that as a triumph for Emotions Day.

Q. James: *There's some vague, personal thing in there. But I don't know what it is, nor do I particularly want to know. Yuck. Can I just skip this assignment?*
A. Aw, emotions can't hurt you. Not with a simple exercise like this. Sometimes emotions are vague, sometimes not. Yet every one counts. If you see a cow in the fog, it's still a cow, not a barn.

How can I persuade you that it is safe to make contact with your own emotions? Must you purchase a tree-shaped room deodorizer and wear it around your neck for the rest of Emotions Day?

Come on, James. Think harmless, contented cows. Then close your eyes and go inside to find some emotions. If you're not sure what to name that feeling inside you, hang around it and ask. Eventually you'll find something that you can name.

Q. Hannah: In my heart chakra there's a pointy place that feels very sharp. Am I good at this or what?
A. Nice try. Soon as you start noticing chakras, you're experiencing from the spirit category of yourself. Energy flows, colors, lights — it's all very interesting. But energy is not the same as emotion.

Point your consciousness differently, that's all. Today you're especially interested in human emotions. Yours.

Q. Jocelyn: My guides tell me that I am feeling angry. Do I get extra points for having the knowledge come from a higher source?
A. Working with your guides is lovely but a completely different skill set from Empath Empowerment. Please instruct your guides to help you some other time, when you ask for their help, which isn't now.

You, as a human being, are in charge here. That's important because you, as a human being, are the one who suffers when STUFF from other people comes into your aura. And only you, not your guides, can give you the skill set of Empath Empowerment.

Do our "Emotional GPS" technique again. Make direct contact, on your own, with your emotions.

Q. Zachary: What if I don't know what to call these emotions? Isn't it enough to feel them without bothering to find names?
A. Feeling directly is good. But if you want to develop skill as an empath, you definitely need to use your words. Once you get into your emotions, you can find plenty of names for them. Just ask, as in our "Emotional GPS" technique.

It's like being back at the ranch, naming pet cattle. At first, you might feel shy. You're tempted to call them all "Rover." But soon you'll find all the names you need. For starters, here are some useful names for basic human emotions:

- Happy
- Sad
- Scared
- Angry

STAMPEDE

Fear not the stampede. If you were really tending a herd of animals that weighed as much as 1,000 pounds each, and they got themselves the notion of running together in some random fashion, this could be severely challenging for you, the cowboy.

But our cows are only a cute analogy.

So what do I mean when I bring up the possibility of a stampede?

Say that you're hanging out with your buddies Jocelyn, Troy and Hannah. Today being Emotions Day, your plan is to "use" your emotions as a way to tilt inner awareness back to yourself. But what if you really don't want to? What if, inside, you're feeling resistance like this?

No, not there. Please, I don't want to do this. Grrrr.

How horrible that I would ever have done this zany experiment and try these stoooopid techniques, for which I would say that I feel the utmost contempt, except that possibly "contempt" might be considered an emotion, and I am not, repeat NOT, going into any emotions.

Why? Because they make me so annoyed and frustrated, that's why.

Notice some emotional words there? Perchance an emotional undertone?

Any strong disinclination to investigate your own emotions is suspect. Frankly, what I suspect is that if you will only take a deep breath and go inside for a moment, you will find emotions galore.

It may be many emotions, stampeding around. Or it could just be one emotion: *Conrad, The Mighty 10-Ton Bull of Fear.*

Remember this saying: "The only thing we have to fear is fear itself."

If you're scared of emotions, that's called "feeling scared." If you're angry about having too many emotions or having too few, either way, that's called "feeling angry." No emotion can kill you. That would be called "death." And death is not an emotion.

YOUR ASSIGNMENT FOR DAY 10

Live a little today. Live on the wild side. Use Emotional GPS whenever you need to. Do it especially if another person is having strong emotions and you're tempted to join in.

Otherwise you're bringing on extra unskilled Empath Merges, which will have dubious value for helping anyone.

Empaths with gifts that don't involve emotion can do this too, you know. You may have the habit of experiencing another person's emotions indirectly.

For instance, let's say that Troy is feeling very upset. If you have Physical Oneness, you might shift into an experience of what that intense emotion does in his body. And, because this is a "oneness" gift, rather than an "intuition" gift, the tension would be felt within your own body as if it really belonged to you.

If you slipped up in this way, you might think that Troy's physical tension was your problem. And soon it would be. (Wakeup Call is the remedy for such problems, remember?)

Whatever your gift(s) as an empath, when someone else's emotions are very intense, you can be pulled into unskilled Empath Merges, taking on STUFF galore.

Don't go there. Make the very slight, subtle shift of consciousness required to turn your gift(s) OFF.

Remember, you don't have to struggle to do this. Nor need you improvise techniques for "coping" or "boundaries" or self-protection. Techniques you're learning with our 30-Day Plan will protect you just fine, and with considerable finesse.

Today, for instance, you're specializing in turning your empath gift(s) OFF by experimenting with Emotions Day. At least three times today, consciously pay attention to what you are feeling here and now. This will prevent unskilled Empath Merges. Besides, it's fun to live among those crazy cows called "emotions."

Day 11. Spiritual Awareness Day

God can help you to become a Skilled Empath. That would be *your* version of God, of course. He or She might be part of a religion that brings you inspiration, comfort, a sense of connection to something bigger than yourself. What if organized religion doesn't appeal? You might prefer what I call "disorganized religion."

Whatever! Something about life is sacred to you, something deeper than people, places and random events. Today you get to enjoy *that* as a way to help you to activate a category of your human self, useful for stopping those unskilled Empath Merges.

Your spiritual team could have a name like this:

- Me, a good Catholic (or Evangelical Christian, or upstanding Buddhist, or faithful Muslim, or devoted Hindu, or nice Jewish girl from New York, etc.)
- Me plus my Higher Power
- Me, who believes most in my family and wants to be strong and healthy for their sake
- Me and my spiritual search for meaning
- Me, enhanced by one super-duper angel committee

JUST A BIT MORE DEMANDING

Many empaths are in a spiritual rut. (As are many non-empaths, too, so no need to sob especially loudly.) If you're in a spiritual rut, you can move out of it. Today! Simply by acting a bit more demanding!

Think of God as a huge ocean of magical healing water. Most people approach God holding a thimble, begging and pleading to let it be filled. Well, today you are invited to approach God with a much bigger container, maybe the size of a gigantic swimming pool, and ask for that to be filled instead.

What, you think God will refuse, groaning "Aw, that's too hard"? We're talking about a spiritual resource that created the whole amazing planet and more.

Whenever you ask God to help your inner life, it's impossible to ask too much. Give yourself permission to ask big. Demand that God give you more than a thimble-sized blessing.

Ask for huge amounts of self-love, self-confidence, spiritual awakening, clarity, personal power. Or choose anything else that will strengthen you.

WHICH FAVORS, WHEN?

Here's another way that you can make life better during Spiritual Awareness Day (and beyond). Starting today, when you find somebody else in trouble, quit acting as if you are the only possible resource. Sadly, unskilled empaths can be really good at thoughts like:

- Gee, I wish I could help.
- I really feel for you.
- If only there were something I, personally, could do.
- If only I could do even more.
- How I wish I could take away that terrible pain/fear/anger/suffering.

Have you been trying to help others in ways like this? 'Fess up. Then, cut it out.

Your heart is in the right place, but — if I may be frank — your technique stinks.

Any of the previous requests will cause you to do a quick, or not-so-quick, unskilled Empath Merge with the troubled person. You'll do this repeatedly, though probably not consciously. Then you'll pick up STUFF from his/her aura and keep it hanging around in your own personal aura for an indefinite amount of time.

Sweet? Yes. Smart? No, not when you can use the "Take It" technique instead.

Next time you're in a situation where someone needs help, first, consider if there is something practical you can do on the level of objective reality, like take out the garbage or send a condolence card. Decide if you really, truly are willing to do this.

Don't volunteer just because another person has a need. And before you volunteer to do anything bigger than sending a card, ask the other person if he or she even wants you to do it, such as, "Would you like me to take out the garbage?"

Volunteering to do *objective* action is just common sense for anyone, empath or not. Now let's get back to the *subjective* part, that old, familiar kind of volunteering so favored by unskilled empaths.

Take It

When you notice that somebody near you is suffering, don't use the old "I'll take it" method of unskilled empath-dom. Substitute this technique.

And speaking of substituting, I will use the name "X" here to represent the person whom you are trying to help. When doing the technique, substitute that name if you know it. Otherwise use a simple description like "that man I just saw on the street."

1. Choose a personal form of God to help you when doing the technique this particular time. For instance you could choose Jesus, Buddha, Kwan Yin, Krishna, Archangel Michael, Archangel Gabriel or Isis.
2. Think the name once.
Notice, the verb is "think," not necessarily "believe in," "worship," "visualize," etc. None of that is necessary for this technique to work properly.
"Think" means say the name once in a normal way. Think this inside your head. Then consider Step 2 as successfully done.
3. Quick as thought, that Divine Being will show up.
No kidding. This statement isn't based just on my personal experience but from teaching this super-easy technique to students in many parts of the world. The Divine Being you have

requested will instantly appear in His or Her body of super-high- vibrational light.

Incidentally, He or She will definitely NOT demand to see your membership card for any particular religious organization.

4. Optional: Inwardly you may sense that Divine Being or feel an emotion like comfort. If you spontaneously find this happening, enjoy it. Doing the "Take It" technique over time, your awareness of Divine presence will grow. Eventually, you will notice that you're not playing pretend with dollies or action figures. Authentic healing really does happen.

5. Think a sentence like this inside your head. "The pain/fear/anger/suffering in X, please take it away, if appropriate."

6. Ask the Divine Being, "Please cut all psychic ties between me and X. Then fill both of us with Divine love, light, and power."

Based on research I have done with students and clients worldwide, I'm convinced that Take It works every time. The Divine Being will remove as much as is possible to remove, which equals at least as much as you, personally, would have removed through an unskilled Empath Merge.

And, of course, no pain is ever removed from the other person without his/her giving permission at the level of the soul.

IT EVEN WORKS FOR ZACHARY

Here's an example of using the "Take It" technique. Say that you're visiting with your pal Zachary when suddenly you notice that he's upset about something. Yes, he's definitely sad.

Now you own the "Take It" technique. So your best way of helping is NOT to share Zachary's sadness. You don't have to "feel for him" since he's already doing a perfectly fine job of being in contact with his own misery.

Instead, talk to Zachie. Find out more about what's going on with him. Then think something like "Merlin. Be here. Please send Zachary help for his sadness, if

appropriate. Now, cut all psychic ties between Zachary and me. Then fill us both with Divine love, light, and power."
Then go back to focusing on The Most Important Person in the Room.

Incidentally, if you happen to be able to see or sense Divine Beings (which I'd love to teach you sometime, but it's outside the scope of this particular book) guess what? You'll notice that STUFF really does leave Zachary. It goes directly into Merlin. Afterwards clean energy comes out the other side of Merlin.

You see, the Ascended Master Merlin (or any other Divine Being) has a different kind of body from us humans. He can help beautifully. He helps with no strings attached. Only He won't usually help without an invitation from someone in human form.

Hey, I didn't make those rules. That's just how it is at Earth School.

Another rule here is that, although asking for help is perfectly fine, you don't have the right to micromanage Divine Beings. "Take it" is fine. So is "Help him," please. However, it would be spiritually tacky to demand something like this:

Take away Zachary's pain by giving him $4 million right now. Then would you please give him the guts to finally quit that job he hates so much? While you're at it, fix his tendency to spoil his kids rotten, because that isn't making his life any easier either. Euww, they are so annoying!

To summarize, the "Take It" technique works just fine, provided you that you co-create rather than try to boss around. You're becoming The Most Important Person in The Room, not The Most Important Person in The Universe.

YOUR ASSIGNMENT FOR DAY 11

Today's assignment is simple.

1. Include three 2-minute periods where you sit, close your eyes, and inwardly make contact with Your Spiritual Team.
2. Experiment at least once with the "Take It" technique

3. Of course, you'll continue with Be Deep as inspired.
4. And, if you notice that you may have picked up STUFF from anyone, soon as possible do the Wakeup Call.

Day 12. Soul Day

Oops, have you forgotten that you have a soul? Most people living today are in that same boat. And life in that boat is harsh!

Before explaining what you can do to improve things, I had better define what I mean by "soul" in the first place.

Soul is different from spirit, although many people mix these terms up. Both begin as a divinely designed chunk of what makes you YOU.

This quirky one-of-a-kind quality has been you since you first were created. The You-ness makes you at least as unique as a snowflake. Since you're not a snowflake but human, that You-ness lasts for longer than the time it takes to thaw. Your individuality is eternal.

For this entire lifetime, your You-ness expresses in two different ways.

Your *spirit* longs to connect back to source. This makes you like E.T. in the Spielberg movie, constantly trying to return back to the mother ship. Okay, maybe you don't walk around whimpering "E.T. phone home." Nonetheless, you have been developing your own methods to phone home, like these:

- Gazing at a beautiful sunset
- Falling in love
- Wishing on a star, a birthday cake, a dandelion
- Eating chocolate
- And all those things that you did yesterday for Spiritual Awareness Day

When the search for spiritual connection works right, it brings great relief. You want that moment to last forever. How human it is, desiring to end the homesickness. How you may yearn to know, beyond the shadow of a doubt, that you are eternally one with God.

By contrast, *soul* is how You-ness expresses because you are human. Some choices make you feel great, others don't. For instance you have:

- Favorite foods (a.k.a. soul food — and for you it doesn't have to be fried chicken and collards)
- Favorite music (a.k.a. soul music — which for you could be polkas, waltzes, whatevers)
- Favorite ways to be affectionate (e.g., soul kiss — enough said)

Living with soul ought to be the most natural thing in the world. Actually, it was… when you were about two years old. Then you learned manners. For better or worse, you learned how to understand words like "should."

Nothing can kill your soul. But if anything came close, surely it would be the word "should."

Don't get me wrong. Doing one's duty is necessary. It makes the world go around at least as much as love does. But consider this: On any given day, how many things do you choose merely because you're supposed to?

Joyless, dutiful, responsible, "adult" behavior. Yech!

Most people don't spend even one hour a day doing what they need and want as human beings.

Take exercise as an example. Do you work out regularly? If so, perhaps you dutifully get on some treadmill. Or do you, instead, pursue a form of exercise that makes you go "Yabba dabba do"? (Substitute words from your personal inner language of bliss. It's one of those very private, soulful things about you.)

Maybe your soul would prefer for you to dance naked around the house.

Lexi would rather practice picking up marbles between her toes.

Zachary would rather stomp around the bedroom, splashing himself with aftershave while he practices grunting.

Have you asked your soul lately which form of exercise would be a whole lot of fun? Or do you do as most adults do, slap a big, bored, virtuous smile on your face as you "get with the program"?

WHY SOUL MATTERS

Researching Soul Thrill has become one of my specialties as an emotional and spiritual healer. Based on researching thousands of auras, I've found that 299 out of 300 people living today aren't living with soul. Anyone can, however.

All it takes is spending one hour each day doing any combo of things that thrill your soul. More than one hour won't hurt. It's just not required.

All you need is that one silly hour, 10 minutes here plus 5 minutes there, etc. With that soul-level minimum daily requirement, an aura becomes better connected at the high heart chakra. Translation: Your soul is being expressed through your everyday human personality. Today you can start becoming that person. Besides making your life more fulfilling, living with soul will help you to become a Skilled Empath.

Why? The Most Important Person in The Room does not spend most waking hours feeling like a galley slave. Fully enjoying yourself in the moment, you'll avoid feeling guilty about focusing on yourself.

Yes, I'm boldly suggesting that one under-reported cause of guilt is simply not having enough fun. When you're having a really good time, you've got some serious momentum going. Guilt can precede or follow a really good time, not happen during. When really enjoying yourself, you're far too busy having fun to doubt yourself.

And you don't have to quit your job to express your soul. Be sneaky about it, if you must, by using the following technique.

Soul at Work

At work, give yourself a five-second soul break occasionally. For instance, do one of these.

• Look around the room until you find a color that really appeals to you. Close your eyes and imagine that a paint bucket

filled with that color is being poured over your head. Let the energy of that color be absorbed wherever your body needs it most.
• Whistle.
• Fill a coffee cup with water, bend upside down, and drink from the far-away edge.
• Daydream about a favorite vacation, past or future.
• Imagine that you have been given five million dollars. Think about one thing FOR YOURSELF that you would do with the money.

Once you start making contact with the category of yourself called "Soul," you'll generate loads of soulful things you can do. At dinner, for instance, eat something really delicious, not merely convenient or virtuous.

If that's not possible, sit somewhere secluded and eat like a kid. Honestly, when was the last time you played with your food? Do you have any idea what you're missing?

Here's another example of soulful lifestyle: Tonight, when you have spare time, don't meekly sit in front of the TV or do the same-old Internet-schtick. Choose something else, something fun.

YOUR ASSIGNMENT FOR DAY 12

Wherever you go during your waking hours today, whoever is there with you, I invite you to somehow make today a golden day, a gusto kind of day. As much as possible, do what makes you happy.

Just don't get yourself fired or arrested.

And when you're with other people today, please, please, oh pretty please:

1. Continue to make yourself The Most Important Person in The Room.
2. Be Deep occasionally.
3. Should you feel as though you're starting to take on anyone else's STUFF, give yourself a Wakeup Call.

Day 13. Bingo

Let me show you how the game of Bingo applies to Empath Empowerment.

A Bingo card contains five categories, famously known as *B.I.N.G.* and *O.* Your inner self contains more than five categories because you are way more exciting than a typical Bingo card. Your inner categories are *Mind.Body.Spirit.Intellect.Soul.Emotions.* and *Environment.*

None of these matters most. I put them in this particular order just because I like the acronym: *MBS. I see!*

In Bingo, there's a Caller who randomly draws one token at a time. It's numbered within a category, like B12 or N43. After a token is called, you check your scorecard to see if your card matches up. Maybe you use a colorful ink dauber to keep track as you go. Accumulate five big, red blobs in a row and you can be the one who stands up screaming, "Me, me, I win. Bingo!"

In the game I call Inner Bingo, who gets to be The Caller? You, nobody else. Besides that, you get to be The Player. (In addition, have you guessed? You just might become The Lucky Winner.)

Inner Bingo

For this self-awareness technique, don't draw out tokens. Stop the action in the scene where you are right now. Lightly, quickly, analyze which of your inner categories has been active. Add percentages if you wish.

Instead of B.I.N.G. and O., your categories are Mind, Body, Spirit, Intellect, Soul, Emotions and Environment. Recognizing *MBS. I see!* can help you to win at the game of life.

Here are examples of how you might win, playing Inner Bingo.

• You're instant messaging Hannah, laughing your head off at her amazing wit and wisdom: Intellect 80%, Emotions 20%
• You're at work, taking a mental health break, contemplating how you might like your job more: Spirit 80%, Soul 10%, Intellect 10%
• Back home, you're cleaning up the kitchen. Darn it, you are bored like crazy. Still, the chore must be done: Mind 100%

However you score, you win just because you are playing. Unlike the other version of Bingo, there's no wasting time with a missed round, where somebody else gets to score and you don't. Whatever you find when you check inside, you will always find at least one active category. So you win.

Besides, very act of self-recognition means something important. You are moving your consciousness on purpose, in an effortless, natural manner. Skill at doing this turns you into The Most Important Person in The Room.

Whenever you shift attention from somebody else to yourself, what else happens? Automatically your empath gift(s) turn OFF. So you stop taking on other people's STUFF.

Re-set! And such a win for you!

Inner Bingo is a here-and-now way to remind yourself of the richness and potential variety of your inner life.

YOUR CATEGORIES FOR INNER BINGO

In the past, you've surely heard the expression "mind-body-spirit." How limiting! During our 30-Day Plan, you've had personal experience with Mind Day, Intellect Day, etc. So you know that you have more to you than those three puny M.B.S. categories. Let's summarize all seven exciting basics of Inner Bingo, your categories of *MBS. I see!*

1. MIND

Your simplest inner functioning, mind is experienced as thoughts. Also, your mind links subjective and objective experience.

2. BODY

Awareness of your physical body could be anything from head to toes, front to back, left to right. You might feel that body at skin-level, in muscles, bones or organs, etc.

3. SPIRIT

Noticing energy, auras, movement, colors or silence — spirit shows up as subtle experiences of any kind within regular reality. For instance, closing your eyes, you might feel as though you become big or small or apparently twirl around.

Can you be feeling things like this even though, physically, you're just sitting still. Sure. And doesn't that make sense? When such things happen, you're not hallucinating, just having a perception from the spirit category... about your physical body.

4. INTELLECT

Complex, sophisticated inner functioning, experienced as thoughts... yet your intellect is different in quality from the simpler kind of thoughts from the mind category. Your intellect includes abilities like *thoughts about thoughts,* creativity, discernment, learning new concepts and multi-tasking.

5. SOUL

You have very personal desires, likes and dislikes, and a keen sense of your own truth. This counts. It even counts as a category. Soul is your most intense and personal experience of yourself as a human being.

6. EMOTIONS

Feelings in this category are expressed with words like happy, sad, scared, angry. A beginner might confuse emotions with other inner experiences, like "Lots of energy" (Spirit) or "Achy" (Body).

How to move from words like these to words that will be more informative about emotions? Ask yourself a question like, "When I am achy right now, how does that make me feel emotionally?"

7. ENVIRONMENT

Whether with others or alone, indoors or outdoors, here and now, you always have a way of being yourself in the environment. The particular version of yourself changes according to the situation, so you act one way with your mother, another with your brother, yet another with your boss at work.

This social version of yourself, here and now, is "Your personal way of being in the environment right now" or "Environment" for short.

Which parts of mind-body-spirit-intellect-soul-emotions-environment are you using when? Today's technique helps you pay attention. You're not changing a thing, simply noticing.

Inner Bingo doesn't need to be more complicated than checking a physical Bingo card. After all, you're well prepared. Earlier assignments from our 30-Day Plan have given you exceptional familiarity with six of your categories.

Only one of these categories hasn't yet been explored yet in depth: Environment. So....

HELLO, ENVIRONMENT

Back when you were an unskilled empath you may have felt reluctant to experience that Environment category. Remember what that was like, 13 days ago?

Often you felt like a chameleon. Typically, you were The Least Important Person in The Room, the invisible one. Other people's versions of Environment could have seemed to trump yours. My, how you have changed already!

As you become even more skilled as an empath, you'll discover new ways to be present in the category of Environment. Have you experienced any of the following changes? (If not yet, expect them soon. Just keep doing your daily assignments.)

1. DRESSING

Unskilled Empath: When other people look at how I'm dressed, I see how they react to me. And that's the main thing I notice. ◆

Skilled Empath: I notice how I'm dressed, and it pleases me.

2. RANDOM VOLUNTEERING

Unskilled Empath: When someone around me like Zachary feels uncomfortable, physically or emotionally. I can't help but notice and wish I could help..

Skilled Empath: I notice how I feel around Zachary. My first loyalty is to myself, not to him. Sometimes I might decide to use the "Take It" technique on him, but I never volunteer to such an extent that I lose the main focus of my life, which is me. Speaking of which....

3. FOCUS

Unskilled Empath: When other people, like Zachary, are around, I can't stay completely focused on what I'm doing. Instead, I pay a lot of attention to what Zachary needs and his opinion of me.

Skilled Empath: I can stay focused on whatever I'm doing, regardless of the opinions of wonderful Zachary. Basically, I have my own way of doing whatever I'm doing in this particular social situation.

4. SELF-AWARENESS

Unskilled Empath: When with other people, like Zachary, I'm very aware of how I could help him, what's going on with him, etc. All that information streams through me, drowning out my sense of self.

Skilled Empath: When with other people, even someone as fascinating as Zachary, that doesn't prevent me from having my own MBS. *I see!* or my personal goals and desires. Zachary may come or go but this is my life. I always come first.

5. SELF-CONFIDENCE

Unskilled Empath: I tend to become who other people think I am.

Skilled Empath: I stay myself, doing what I do, feeling as I feel, unapologetically being the way I am.

Brave Explorer, putting yourself first can be fun. Not wicked fun, human fun. Inner Bingo helps you sort out the kind of fun you are having.

6. SEXUAL CONFIDENCE

Actually, you could interpret all you just read about Environment for a Skilled Empath in terms of sexiness. In any environment where there's a chance for sex, Skilled Empaths will appear sexier than unskilled empaths. We're more fully present.

Unskilled Empath: I tend to feel only as sexy as other people think I am.

Skilled Empath: I stay sexually confident, doing what I do, feeling as I feel, unapologetically being who I am.

YOUR ASSIGNMENT FOR DAY 13

Play Inner Bingo at least five times. At random intervals, pause inwardly, close your eyes and notice:

- Among your seven categories, which ones are most active right now, mind, body, spirit, intellect, soul, emotions or environment?
- Approximate the percentage for each. Make note on a pad of paper, your Blackberry, wherever you like.

No need to be precise or fix the math so your score adds up to a perfect 100%. Nor does this technique require that you change a thing. You're simply learning about yourself, specifically your habits for using mind-body-spirit-intellect-soul-emotions-environment.

Make a guess, right now, what Inner Bingo will show you today.

Think that you will use the same category of self, over and over? During a full set of waking hours, might you use 3, 5 or all 7?

Find out, because you might be pleasantly surprised. Regardless, the very act of playing Inner Bingo will strengthen you as an empath.

Day 14. Advanced Bingo

Yesterday you started playing Inner Bingo, catching yourself at random moments, then noticing which categories of self were most active. Did you find yourself favoring one or two categories out of habit (like Intellect, Spirit, Mind or Environment)? Then let's help you become more resourceful as a person by adding the technique I call "Advanced Bingo."

Perhaps you don't need that kind of help. Maybe your assignment yesterday showed that you're already using your full set of categories. The technique you learn today still can help you, because it's so useful for dealing with people who are draining.

- Say that your plans for today involve spending time with your friend Jocelyn, and she happens to be very depressed. If you engage with her by living mainly from the Emotions category, that could spell trouble. Instead, for part of your visit, use Advanced Bingo to move into a different part of yourself, such as Mind, Soul or Body. Not only will you feel better. You'll find it far easier to keep your empath gift(s) nicely turned OFF.
- Similarly, you could be living mostly from Body awareness but you decide to change that while hanging out with Roscoe. Why? He's such a fierce hypochondriac.
- Or how about dealing with Hannah? Mostly she's a fabulous friend but her intellect is on overdrive. If you follow her lead and shift into living mostly from Intellect, her headache could soon become your own.

For Advanced Bingo to work, you don't have to assess other people the way I just did. You don't need to figure out how they emphasize one category of life or another.

Remember, the skill set for Empath Empowerment is supposed to be effective but *easy*. Let simple discomfort be your cue: "What, I'm starting to feel uncomfortable hanging out with Roscoe? Time to do Advanced Bingo!"

Soon as you start feeling drained by another person, do our latest technique.

Advanced Bingo

To play Advanced Bingo, reach inside the token tumbler of yourself (one quick thought does it) and pull out N37. I mean Body awareness, Mind awareness or some other personal kind of awareness that is different from the category you have been using before.

Give just the tiniest inner nudge to your inner self. Your consciousness will do all the rest.

I want to emphasize how really easy Advanced Bingo can be. Our 30-Day Plan has familiarized you with all the categories of yourself. More strongly than before, you "own" each of them. It's your *MBS. I see!* So you can use this however you wish.

As for the amount of effort necessary for our new technique, it's ridiculously teensy. Has this ever happened to you? Playing regular Bingo, you need just one particular token pulled so that you can win. Inside you're yelling, pushing hard, "Pick N37, N37. I must have N37."

Only the tiniest fraction of that effort is needed to play Advanced Bingo and win. Soon as you choose Body rather than Mind or Intellect, etc., bam! You've got it! Just one quick thought. Inwardly, you can be all body, all whatever, all the time — at least for the next few minutes.

Say that you choose to bring awareness to the Body category. Suddenly you will start noticing all sorts of interesting things about your left foot, your nasal passages, whatever seems new and fascinating in the world of My Personal Body Sensations. A fine show it is!

BEING THERE FOR JOCELYN

Just because Advanced Bingo is easy, don't underestimate its power to keep you clear as an empath. In this example, your friend Jocelyn is upset over something and you're being there for her, as any good friend would. Did you ever consider the meaning of that common expression, "Being there for someone"? That can be done very suavely right on the surface of life.

What is required to satisfy the social and moral requirement for "being there" for someone like Jocelyn? Physically be present. Listen to her words. Show a sympathetic attitude.

This is all non-empaths do, "being there" for someone. Only empaths are wacky enough to routinely interpret "Being there for her" like this:

*   *Unconsciously, I will merge with Jocelyn's aura 30 super-quick times in 10 minutes, lifting STUFF from her aura and depositing it into mine.*
*   *Consciously I will push myself to become very, very deeply involved.*
*   *I will give as much energy to Jocelyn as possible... until she tells me she's satisfied.*
*   *At the end of the hour, I will charge her the standard rate for psychiatric services.*

Just kidding about that last part.

Back at you now, as a Skilled Empath. Thanks to Advanced Bingo, you can act just like any non-empath, "being there" for Jocelyn by outwardly going through the motions. Thanks to Advanced Bingo, you stay free of her STUFF. Thus, you can act like a good friend yet remain The Most Important Person in The Room.

STILL THE MOST IMPORTANT PERSON

Repeat after me, "How much must I give to *anyone* before I deserve to consider myself The Most Important Person in The Room? Nothing!"

Forget about Advanced Bingo for a moment. Forget, even about Jocelyn, fascinating though her sorrows might be. Instead imagine that George Clooney (or whichever celebrity you prefer) has just entered the room. Assume that nothing else has changed about the place where you are.

Don't you think you might, constantly, be very aware of George, no matter what else is happening?

Sighting a movie star when you're out walking, dining at your neighborhood Burger King, shopping at the mall, etc., most otherwise "normal" people would act star struck. They would stare. And sweat. And babble, "Omigod, I'm in the room with George Clooney. George Clooney, for crying out loud !!!!!!!!!!!!!!!!!!!!"

Yet meaning no insult to the fabulous Mr. Clooney, why should he be any more important to you than you? All I'm asking you to do today is to treat yourself like The Most Important Person in The Room, even if that room contains Swooney Clooney.

So there you are with Jocelyn and you happen to be paying attention to the Body category of your mind-body-spirit-intellect-soul-emotions-environment.

Right now, that might mean weighing and balancing physical sensations in both your earlobes. Does one happen to feel just a bit heavier right now? Hmmm, how fascinating is that?

By now Jocelyn is sobbing. If all that you offer her now is "being there" (along with paying quality attention to yourself, Body-Day style) are you being a good enough friend? Sure you are. Let's count the ways:

- You are keeping Jocelyn company.
- You are nodding at the appropriate intervals.
- You are letting Jocelyn talk to her heart's content.
- You are handing out tissues, as needed.

Besides that, being well on your way to behaving like a Skilled Empath, you can give Jocelyn the wonderful gift of our Take It technique.

Remember, when you notice especially large chunks of pain, rage or worry pouring out of Jocelyn, you can think, "Archangel Raphael, take it." Thus, you bring healing galore, without having to process it through your own personal aura.

When your visit with Jocelyn finally ends, and you have kept your empath gift(s) turned OFF the whole time, you won't feel like one of Jocelyn's used tissues. You will be vibrant, healthy, and ready for your next social encounter, whether or not it includes George Clooney. (Sigh!)

YOUR ASSIGNMENT FOR DAY 14

Just like yesterday, play Inner Bingo five random times. Only today, you'll do one thing differently. Add Advanced Bingo as needed:

If you notice that one category (like Emotions) is being favored again and again, substitute paying attention to some different category.

By now you know, shifting your consciousness is easy. Whenever you wish, you can choose a different category of experience, whether mind, body, spirit, intellect, soul, emotions or your personal way of being in this environment. One quick thought will do it, so familiar have you become with all of your inner categories as a person.

Play Advanced Bingo today and watch your life improve.

Day 15. Say Whatever

Brave Explorer, you have been doing great at using all your categories as a person, mind-body-spirit-intellect-soul-emotions-environment. All of these count as *subjective* resources for being a Skilled Empath.✦ Today let's start to introduce some *objective* resources: Speech and action.

As an aura reader, I've noticed that many empaths carry a huge amount of clog in their throat chakras. Could you be at risk?

UNCLOGGING, LIFE'S EASIEST DANCE

I love watching those Irish Riverdance cloggers as much as you do but, please, save the big tapping shoes for your feet. Not your neck.

Clogging up your throat chakra doesn't feel like dancing. It happens in situations like these:

- Much as you enjoy being with Meg, you resent how she treats you. Frustrated, you say nothing. Great job, except for your throat chakra!
- Troy talks. And talks. And talks. Politely, you hide your boredom. Unbeknownst to you, your prize for this great success at hiding is new STUFF in your throat chakra.
- Although you disagree with Lexi as she goes on a rant, you avoid telling her so. So important to be polite! So unimportant, honoring all the things you have to say! So much clog coming into you, staying long after Lexi leaves the room!
- How you wish that, for once, James would quit bothering you. You wish. You don't say. And, therefore, you clog

yourself up. Long after James has stopped trying to make you angry, the STUFF will keep doing that job just fine.

Why is it, people talk about "Stifling a yawn" yet never mention the deeper problem, "Stifling a throat chakra"?

Admittedly, most folks today wouldn't say this because they don't know what the heck a "chakra" is. A chakra is part of your aura. That is a collection of energy bodies around your physical body, full of information.

An aura's information is especially concentrated in *chakras,* places that correspond to your physical body. Think of a healthy aura as containing free-flowing energy. How can that energy flow properly when a chakra contains globs and blobs of stuck energy, what I call "clog" or "STUFF"?

When you swallow your words, that energy doesn't just go away. One common sign of throat clog is....

DELICIOUS SARCASM

Yesterday I saw these words on a tee-shirt: *"Sarcasm is just one of many fine services I offer."*

I giggled to myself in a cool, post-modern sort of way. But then I went "Aha!" and designed the following assignment for you (and for me):

Sarcasm Fast

Could we possibly cut out the excess irony? Just for one day? Are you brave enough to join me in a Sarcasm Fast? Then, just for today:

1. If you hear *someone else* being sarcastic, sing "Thank God, I'm a country boy." Wait, that's not it. Think, "Gee, that was sarcasm."
2. Learn from the sarcasm. Ask yourself, "Did he/she use the sarcasm to express something or to keep from expressing something?" (The latter, of course, would add more throat chakra clog.) Even without being a fully qualified aura reader, or turn-

---

ing a single empath gift ON, I'll bet you can tell the difference. Most sarcasm adds to throat chakra clog.

3. If *you* feel the urge to say something sarcastic, don't.

4. Oops, if that thought comes too late, because a sarcastic remark has already left your mouth, ask yourself, "Did I use that sarcasm to express something effectively? Or was that sarcasm a signal that I just clogged up my throat chakra?"

5. Is there something not sarcastic that you could say in this situation? It might be as simple as, "Excuse me?" or any Throat Unclogger Sentence. (These Unclogger Sentences will be discussed soon.) Just do it!

Break the speech clog habit one day at a time, one situation at a time. When you feel tempted, take a deep breath and ask yourself, "If it were safe to say whatever I wanted right now, what would it be?" For instance:

- What a nasty, ignorant thing you've just done.
- I couldn't disagree with you more, you nitwit.
- Your expression/words/behavior/body odor just hurt my feelings.

Do I recommend that you then come out directly with words like these? Of course not. Nothing in this book is meant to get you fired, arrested, or divorced.

However, I am going to ask you to speak just a bit of your truth. Say enough to remove that bit of throat chakra clog.

Throat Unclogger Sentences

What if part of you says "Without sarcasm, no way"? Then tell yourself, "Way." Try injecting a Throat Unclogger Sentence, like one of the following, into your conversation:

- Excuse me, but are you aware that you just ....?
- What an interesting point of view! My opinion is different.
- What did you mean by that?

> Throat Unclogger Sentences can also be helpful if you have
> communication problems other than sarcasm, such as shyness,
> awkwardness in front of strangers, powerlessness, feeling left
> out or disconnected from a group of people, not knowing how
> to do intimacy.

Alas, our three simple sentences won't completely solve all life's problems. (Surprise me, though. If this should happen, write a Guest Post for my blog, www.rose-rosetree.com/blog. Share the miracle, because this would really be a miracle.)

Although miracles are always welcome, our goal here is humbler. Master the part of Empath Empowerment that involves unclogging your throat chakra.

Guess what I have learned about Throat Unclogger Sentences, like the examples above?

All it takes is one tiny non-sarcastic sentence to avoid adding the latest bit of gunk to your throat chakra.

Remember, the words are for your benefit, not the other person's. Say you're complaining to James. Maybe he won't even answer. Well, that would be information for you about give-and-take in your relationship. If James does respond in a friendly way, you will have gently begun a discussion (and maybe started to upgrade your relationship).

Whatever the outcome, for the sake of your effectiveness in objective life, it's important to open up your throat chakra. That part of your aura is a vital connector between you and other people. Speaking up for yourself is essential for skill as an empath.

YOUR ASSIGNMENT FOR DAY 15

If you know that you have absolutely no throat clog whatsoever, you get the day off. Otherwise, dare to experiment. Just for today, Brave Explorer, avoid all sarcasm. Use Throat Unclogger Sentences. And, for lifelong Empath Empowerment, remember this:

Every day from now on, in every situation, you can find a safe way to speak at least a little bit of your truth.

Day 16. Turn Life Inside Out

Brave Explorer, you are becoming *oh so good* at expressing yourself effectively. How can I reward you?

Allow me to present you with a brand new way to slice-and-dice reality: When was the last time you paid attention to one big, fascinating choice that everyone gets to make from moment to moment?

Choose One Reality at a Time

At any given time, you have a choice. Which reality will you favor, the objective version or the subjective one? Being human, you can only choose one at a time.

• Objective Reality is what happens in life, like the *front* section of a newspaper.

• Subjective Reality is how you feel about what happens, like the *feature* section of a newspaper.

Making the choice can be as simple as any other slight shift of emphasis. Choose. Aim your consciousness. Automatically you'll switch one on, the other off.

You can tell them apart, right? Objective Reality and Subjective Reality are hardly identical twins.

Every human has been wired to appreciate both... and conveniently both sides of life can always be found in the here and now. Yet often a person will get out of balance and forget that life contains both Objective and Subjective Reality. For example:

- Curmudgeonly Roscoe can act sooo over-objective. He jokes, "What do you mean I hurt your feelings? Show me the bruises."
- Jocelyn means well. But she acts way over-subjective. "I can't go to work today. I'm not in the right kind of mood."

Here's a long-overdue announcement for Roscoe and his pals: Hurt feelings are subjective but real.

And here's some news for the Jocelyns of the world: Most paying jobs aren't done on the basis of "I'm in the mood." With most jobs, you're supposed to follow an external schedule.

Clocks are a great example of Objective Reality. And one useful thing about having a job, any job, is how it helps remind you to notice Objective Reality.

Many empaths who think, "I hate my job," really hate Objective Reality.

OBJECTIVE OR SUBJECTIVE?

If you have been over-subjective, let's start changing that now.

What if you're already great at balancing Objective Reality and Subjective Reality? Then today is your golden opportunity to notice what other people do. Skilled empaths need to thoroughly understand this kind of balance. Observe people in any given situation. Do they stay balanced? Or do they favor one reality over the other?

Everyone, not just empaths, can develop the habit of acting over-subjective. It's especially tempting for empaths, however, since we have such profound insights into others.

Sometimes we pay so much attention to what's happening with people's inner lives that we forget to notice objective reality. Consequently it becomes impossible for us to take effective action.

A subjective approach to problem solving would be trying to influence someone else's energy, feelings, thinking, etc. Earth School isn't set up for people to use this approach unless it is a designated session for psychotherapy, aura healing, etc.

Instead, the effective (and socially acceptable) way to interact with people involves objective skills, like speech and action.

WHAT IS WRONG WITH THIS STORY?

This story illustrates the difference between subjective vs. objective action for problem solving. Joyce is a student of mine who has made huge progress since recounting this frustrating experience.

"On Saturday morning, Marissa came by to visit. That was fine with me. I was expecting her.

For the first two hours, I was really enjoying myself. Then I began to wish she would go home. But Marissa stayed. And she stayed. And she stayed.

"I went through every emotion you can imagine. I felt bored, resentful, depressed, you name it.

"After six hours, my prayers were finally answered. Marissa went home."

You do appreciate the preventable part, right? Joyce was so over-subjective, it made her powerless. Paying extra attention to inner agony didn't solve Joyce's problem. Nor was it necessary to drag God into her mess.

To end the unwelcome visit, she needed an objective solution.

All Joyce needed to do was say these magic words, "Marissa, thanks for visiting but now it is time go home."

Okay, because you got the point so well, let me reward you with an even more extreme story about objective-subjective balance.

INSPIRATION AT THE SUBWAY CRASH

The following story was told triumphantly by Hiroyuki during a workshop for empaths that I gave in Tokyo.

"For years, I've had a job that I don't especially like. To get there, I take the J-R Subway line. You may know that this subway line has problems with cars crashing into the trains. Many people are killed every year.

"Last week, my train had another one of these fatalities. We passengers had to stand around and wait for a very long time until the subway got moving again. Well, as I sat there waiting, I received a very important spiritual insight.

"All those people dying — that was just God's way of giving me a message. I need to get a new job. Something closer to home!"

Many empaths are deeply spiritual people. So we look for signs. Well, everything that happens does NOT have to be a sign… or carry any other big subjective meaning.

The constant search for meaning can be a way to slow down your evolution.

Ironic, isn't it?

Every life event, every burp, every wilted flower, every death in your vicinity — that does not have to be interpreted as a cosmic sign created expressly for you.

HOW MANY STREETS MUST YOU CLEAN?

I was born and raised in New York City. Exciting though The Big Apple may be, let's face it. Other cities in the world are cleaner.

At one point in my development, as I walked down the street, I would take personal responsibility for cleaning up litter along my route.

I was there for a reason, right?

How I walked definitely wasn't a marathoner's speed: One step. Then stop and pick up old beer cans. Then grab a soggy paper bag with food leftovers dripping out. Go to the trash can and come back. Take three more baby steps in my intended direction. Then back down to clean up more garbage.

Eventually, I realized that I needed to focus on my particular journey, my destination. It didn't have to be my job in life to pick up other people's trash wherever I went.

Other people's trash, I realized, could be just that, trash. Not a cosmic message that I had to stop and interpret and fix.

No matter how much you wish to serve humanity, God has given you only so many hours in the day. Constantly looking for signs is a sure way to lose your focus in life and become over-subjective.

Doing this, you will miss about 50% of your life (the objective part, the accomplishing part). Instead, you can have a spiritually meaningful life that is also balanced.

Fixing a problem like this can be simple. Just use your God-given ability to be objective as well as subjective. The following technique can help.

Reboot Your Inner Computer

Think of yourself as a computer, an empathic one. You contain software for perfect balance of objective and subjective life. But maybe you haven't been using that program.

Here is a sentence you can say out loud to reboot your computer and switch on that program for Objective-Subjective Balance.

"I automatically balance the subjective and objective sides of my life, effective right now."

Why bother to say these words out loud? If you just think them, results will be limited to the subjective circuits within you. Speaking out loud produces real, live sound waves that bounce around in the objective world.

Yelling isn't required. In fact you could simply whisper the words. But if you want this reboot to work, definitely speak the words aloud in some way. You'll be rewarded with an effortless shift into Objective-Subjective Balance.

What I love most about this tiny technique is how effectively it works. No effort is required beyond saying that one sentence aloud. Your subconscious mind and aura will respond automatically because that balancing program really has been installed deep within you by the Cosmic Computer Programmer.

For extra help during Day 16, write these words on a reminder card: *"I automatically balance the subjective and objective sides of my life, effective right now."*

Read it aloud to improve your Objective-Subjective Balance. You'll gain results in both spheres of life — more effectiveness in outer life plus more inner serenity.

YOUR ASSIGNMENT FOR DAY 16

Oh Mighty Most Important Person in The Room, is there no end to your powers? Well, shucks, there might be some, objectively. But could you also have way more Superhero-like power than you have been using? Our assignments for today will help you find out.

1. Reboot your inner computer at will. Use your reminder card to help you.
2. When you encounter a problem today, big or small, don't go over-subjective. Describe the problem objectively. Then search around for something you can say or do to improve things. Objectively.
3. Notice Objective-Subjective Balance in the people you meet. Hopefully, everyone has a firm grasp on reality. But is it mainly a subjective reality or what?

For instance, being with your buddy James, notice what he talks about. Is his conversation mainly about objective reality or the subjective kind? Or might he manage to balance the two?

You can definitely balance them. So what if your habit has been otherwise? All Skilled Empaths must balance the subjective and objective sides of life. It's simply a matter of choice.

Day 17. The Magic Formula

Why isn't it smart to shoot an ant with a cannon?

Probably you don't own even one cannon, while you possess several ants. Wait, that's not the main answer. It involves math:

- Cannon way big.
- Ant way small.

Oh, those silly ant smashers! You may giggle at their foolish ways. Yet for years now, could you have been doing something similar? Here's a hint. Ant-with-cannon syndrome involves the difference between Objective Reality and Subjective Reality.

What did you notice about objective versus subjective when you did your homework yesterday? (Yes, you did that homework, right? Gentle reminder here: To get the best results from this book, take the tiny 10 minutes per day and do your homework. Since we're now on Day 17, you have less than half the book to go. Make the most of our 30-Day Plan.)

Okay, assuming that you did your homework — so you don't have to go back and repeat Day 16 — did you perhaps discover any of the following to be true?

- To solve everyday problems, you can't depend only on subjective insights. Instead you need to take objective action.
- History lesson: When facing problems, wasn't your old habit — as an unskilled empath — to go over-subjective? Instead of taking objective action, did you spend way more time feeling, thinking or analyzing? If so, how well did that work for you?

- Now that you've noticed which people in your life tend to go over-objective, stop. Think. How do you feel about those people? Hint: They may be precisely the folks who have disrespected you, earning your dislike in return. Also, they may be precisely the folks who used to make you feel powerless. Hoo boy, that powerlessness is about to change. As of today!

- Shifting into objective mode from subjective mode wasn't difficult, once you tried it, right? Just like any of the other shifts you have learned to make with our 30-Day Plan, you found an inner tipping point of consciousness, a simple choice. When you make the shift from subjective to objective, it's as natural as wishing on a star. If anything, it's easier. Your inner self isn't light years away but here and now.

Dealing with real-life problems and people who treat you badly, try this one simple way to become far more effective: When you're with them, stop emphasizing your subjective reactions. Favor objective mode instead.

Shooting an ant with a cannon won't get you precision results. Better to use an ant-sized revolver, or whatever weapon is right-sized for your battle.

The Magic Formula

Would Merlin approve? Would Dr. Phil? Who cares? Try the following formula and you'll find it solves many objective-subjective problems like magic.

When somebody in your life is upsetting you, pay attention to the objective circumstances. Then speak about them this way:

1. When you do X…
2. I feel Y.
3. So please do Z.

Finally a use for that high school algebra! Obviously, you can substitute real, meaningful words for xyz, naming specifics about the situation that bothers you. For instance:

1. Zachary, when you use your fingers instead of potato chips to scoop up my onion dip…
2. I feel grossed out. I made this dip for everyone here at the party, not just you and your fingers.
3. Would you please use potato chips from now on? Or ask me. I'll be glad to get you a spoon and plate.

Notice? My lofty example includes humble problem-solving tools like plates. Many situations that bother empaths can be solved with simple, objective things like time, spoons, personal belongings, money, physical bodies, what a person literally says and does.

BALANCED FRIENDSHIP

Beware: When you use The Magic Formula, sometimes so-called "friends" may disappear. Except if this happens, they weren't really friends.

Here's a tale about my friendship with Rhonda. Back in the day, we were both new mothers with no relatives living closer than 200 miles away. Our husbands were great but we needed mom time, conversations when we could discuss our parenting troubles. Soon we became best friends, talking on the phone for an hour most days.

Eventually I began to notice something was wrong. I felt upset, resentful, used somehow. At first I didn't know why. Once I shifted into objective mode, I found the problem easily. Every conversation of ours followed the same pattern, 55 minutes about Rhonda and her problems, then 5 minutes about mine. Soon as I got started, Rhonda would politely end the conversation.

After my Aha!, the very next day, during my five minutes, I said:

1. "Rhonda, I've been noticing a pattern to our conversations. You talk for 55 minutes and then I get to talk for 5.

2. "That doesn't seem fair to me.

3. "Could we try an experiment? You can always go first. Really. But do you think maybe we could try having you talk for 30 minutes and then I could talk for 30?"

That was my last phone conversation with Rhonda. Ever. She wouldn't return my calls. From bosom, breastfeeding buddies to zilch, instantly!

Actually, there's just a bit more to this story. Years later, Rhonda and I met at a party given by a mutual friend who thought we still were close friends. I was thrilled. Only the tiniest apology would have been enough for me to joyfully resume the friendship.

So I ran over to Rhonda. "How I've missed you!" I said, tearing up.

Folding her arms, she gazed at me coldly and said. "Uh-huh."

I went home and cried for 10 days. But I also sorted out the true nature of our friendship. From my side, it had been a friendship. Because I needed a new-mom friend so desperately, I had been content to receive very little. Subjectively, I had made much of that little. From Rhonda's side, however, it hadn't been a friendship so much as a taking. For her, I had been mostly a convenience.

What will *you* find when you use The Magic Formula on a friendship? Maybe you and your friend will fix the problem. Or maybe you'll lose a taker-in-masquerade. Either way you'll gain something valuable.

YOUR ASSIGNMENT FOR DAY 17

Brave Explorer, your assignment today is to use The Magic Formula as appropriate in your personal life. What if your relationships are so perfect that you have no need at all for this kind of problem solving? Do a trial run on people you observe having problems.

For example, waiting in line at the convenience store, you might see a downtrodden spouse being bullied by his S.O. Speak up on behalf of this sad person. Except do this only in private and out of hearing range of anyone at the convenience store.

Certainly do not, under any circumstances, use The Magic Formula on a work relationship, not until you have practiced using these words many times and you're ready to take the consequences.

Skilled Empaths don't shoot ants with cannons. Using your power in the objective world — for many empaths, that is a new approach and takes some practice. In the subjective realm you were born powerful. Go forth today and use your power in the objective realm, too.

Day 18. Gusto

When rockets are launched, they burn big fuel twice. The first blast-off gets the rocket airborne. Later, a second-stage rocket must burn its own special fuel to move the spacecraft out of the earth's atmosphere.

Consider this our perfect analogy for your progress at becoming The Most Important Person in The Room. Becoming a Skilled Empath, there are two phases for blasting off. Phase One involved your first enthusiasm over Empath Empowerment.

Wow! Boom! You had liftoff!

This flashy phase was fueled by self-discovery. Receiving those first easy benefits toward becoming a Skilled Empath, it was tempting to think that you understood enough. Dilettantes and superficial learners will have quit reading this book by now. But not you, Brave Explorer. I can tell because you're still here with me.

That means you have moved forward enough for your second-stage rocket, Phase Two. It is fueled by determination to *live* the benefits of Empath Empowerment.

To move forward, you need to release a second-stage rocket by *blasting through deep resistance*. Yes, deep resistance is a hidden obstacle that empaths must move through before becoming truly skilled.

BLAST OFF BIGGER

Why would deep resistance be a factor? Empath Empowerment involves more than concepts, techniques and homework assignments, much as (I know that) you love them. (Ha! Sarcasm is allowed again today.)

What if you have been living mainly through one of the seven categories of Advanced Bingo? For instance:

- All emotions, all the time — that's my motto.
- Everything can be understood through my intellect (supposedly).
- Spirituality has me living higher than Rapunzel's tower

What's wrong with feeling or thinking that full-blooded earth reality is beneath you? Nothing... in theory. Everything... in habit.

Remember that classic line from the movie called "The Sixth Sense"? A psychic boy (played by Haley Joel Osment) tells his psychologist (played by Bruce Willis), "I see dead people.... Walking around like regular people. They don't see each other. They only see what they want to see. They don't know they're dead."

Not for a moment does it occur to the Bruce Willis character that *he* might be among the clueless dead.

Well, discovering that you've been trapped in just one category (e.g., emotions, intellect or spirit) can be a shock. Not as bad as learning, like Bruce, that you're a ghost! More like hearing that you've got bad breath.

Fortunately, there can be a sweet-smelling solution to any of these problems of emphasis for human life, a solution at least as thrilling as walking on the moon. It's called *walking on earth.*

Skeptical that you might have hidden resistance to walking on earth? Here's a recent client story to illustrate how empaths can be stuck without knowing it.

USING METAPHYSICS TO REMAIN STUCK

Last year, Suzanne asked me for an Aura Report. This is a brief reading where my client sends a photo. I sample seven different chakra databanks, summarizing what I find about gifts of the soul and STUFF.

Tactfully, I explained to Suzanne that she wasn't living with much balance. Her Third Eye Chakra databanks about spirituality were vastly bigger than other parts of her aura. Suzanne took the news well. Months later, she scheduled an appointment.

"Woo-hoo," I thought. "Using techniques of Energy Spirituality, I can help Suzanne to remove large amounts of STUFF, which will help her rebalance."

But no, Suzanne wanted a reading rather than a healing. She had prepared beautifully, I'll admit, listing activities of interest. Unfortunately, all of them were about spirituality, like doing yoga or practicing Reiki or reading spiritual books.

In keeping with Suzanne's request, I supplied detailed feedback. Repeatedly I described how her big growth area was everything but the spiritual practices that enthralled her. "Please pay attention to other aspects of your life," I pleaded.

After several months, Suzanne contacted me again. She wanted a new Aura Report to validate all the progress she was making. I asked her to consider a session of healing instead.

But no. Suzanne was sure that visualizations, prayers, etc. had made all the difference in the world. She wanted me to describe her vastly strengthened aura.

Alas, Suzanne's aura was just as stuck as before. She emailed me, "Oh well, I guess I should have taken your advice and applied the fee for this Aura Report toward a session of Aura Healing. I don't think I know what it feels like to be grounded."

I'm rooting for Suzanne. Her willingness to choose healing next time suggests that, in her own way, she is overcoming resistance to change. (Except I should note that nine months after first-drafting this chapter, here I am editing merrily away when I realize that, oops! Suzanne still hasn't scheduled that session.)

Anyway, let's find out right now if *you* have been dealing with deep resistance to living on earth. For every one of our Cast of Characters who is an empath, there can be a different kind of deep resistance. Some examples follow. Can you recognize yourself in any of the descriptions that follow?

THE FEELING LIFE

Zachary is more sensitive than he looks. Unless with trusted friends, he keeps quiet. When he does talk, it's mostly about emotions:

- Who is good, who isn't — based on Zachary's emotions
- How today goes, based on Zachary's emotions
- Personal growth, in terms of Zachary's emotions

Is anything wrong with being so emotionally aware? Nothing's wrong, except for all the categories of human life that are being ignored.

How much does Zachary learn from what happens in his environment (a.k.a., objective life events)? Unless major drama ensues, Zachary notices only emotions.

Physical body — has that been glimpsed recently? Yes, except Zachary only cares about how he *feels* about that body.

Could there be mindfulness? Sure, Zachary pays attention to his emotions all day long.

Intellectual activity? Being a bright guy, Zachary can tell you precisely how he feels about different ideas.

Spiritual life? Ask Zachary and he'll gladly tell you his feelings about religion and spirituality.

Soul connection? To Zachie, soul is whatever makes him feel happy, nothing more.

YOUR ASSIGNMENT FOR DAY 18
If you are like Zachary

What will help you move into a fuller experience of life? Go back to Days 7-14. Do each of these chapters in turn, one day at a time. Except skip Day 10, Emotions Day. Be proud of the A+ you've already earned there.

Why repeat the assignments for all those days? It's not that last time you did the assignments *wrong*. You're just becoming capable of doing them *better*. And here's the one thing I want you to do *differently* this time around: Gusto.

While you're enjoying your experience of Body Day, etc., congratulate yourself often. Tell yourself, "Ooh la la." (Substitute your favorite term for gusto.) Basically, you're reminding yourself, "This aspect of life is good. I can enjoy myself here."

ALL FIGURED OUT

Hannah is such a brain. She has figured out just about everything and everyone. Now that she understands all our previous chapters about Empath Empowerment, she may be tempted to skim through the rest of the book and not bother doing the exercises.

Big mistake, Hannah!

According to an old proverb, "The eyes can see everything but the eyes." Similarly, mighty though Hannah's brain may be, her intellect cannot warn her about getting stuck in her intellect. But there's hope. Hannah can recognize her problem by reading the following. (Can she — or you — relate?)

Participating in her social environment? Hannah's an expert. She can psych out any conversation, deconstructing power struggles with ease and supplying the subtexts for every speaker. After a conversation, Hannah can easily summarize what she has learned. But does she ever make human contact without bringing along that detached figure-out-er? Maybe not.

Physical body present? If you ask Hannah to notice her body, she can tell you plenty. Oboy, so much she can tell you — about her health, or maybe medical facts, or how a person should eat properly. Alas, feeling sensations within her own body is another, far distant, story.

Would mindfulness be of interest? Hannah definitely gets the concept of mindfulness. So what's new and interesting? Certainly it's not her mind, with its dull recycling of concepts Hannah already knows. Boring!

Emotions anyone? Emotional intelligence may be a point of pride for Hannah. Naming emotions for anyone, herself included, Hannah displays brilliant accuracy. But how about *experiencing* an emotion directly without analyzing it? That's for babies, right?

Spiritual life is a snap. Hannah may think herself quite the authority. Or, maybe, she has decided that spirituality is trivial.

Either way, Hannah could be plenty evolved but will stay a cosmic underachiever with her current habits.

What does it mean to feel a soul connection? For Hannah, "soul" means "thinking about things."

That's true, for her, for now. Only "soul" could mean a whole lot more. The following assignment could make that happen.

YOUR ASSIGNMENT FOR DAY 18
If you are like Hannah

What could help you to blast beyond deep resistance? Go back to Days 7-14. Do each of these chapters in turn, one day at a time, except skip Day 9, Intellect Day.

Resisting that assignment? You know you're smart. Everyone does. They will respect you even more when you use categories of yourself beyond that mighty brain. So often, when people are stuck we try *harder*, rather than *differently*.

Here comes your exercise in "differently." Last time you did Days 7-14 just fine. Here comes your chance to re-do these chapters and learn nothing new whatsoever.

Imagine, no intellectual discoveries needed. Instead, be sloppy and silly and go for pure gusto.

Which means what, exactly? While you're enjoying your experience of Body Day, etc., congratulate yourself. Say "Eureka!" (Substitute your favorite term for gusto.) Remind yourself, "I can relax and enjoy myself here. Afterwards I'll still be smart."

GOING SPIRITUAL

Back to our analogy about lifting off with a second-stage rocket, unless the launch site is stable, you can't go anywhere. A strong platform is needed to thrust against, and James never has valued that platform.

God love him, James is such a devoted spiritual seeker. He neglects everything else but spirit, forgetting that Earth School was created the way it is for a reason. Every component of his mind-body-spirit-intellect-soul-emotions-environment is valuable for spiritual evolution.

Therefore, even for the sake of his service to others as a Skilled Empath, James needs to overcome his comforting old tendency to "go spiritual."

I'm a good one to help with this problem because I spent a good two decades of my life addicted to going spiritual whenever possible.

Everything had to be about God... or my spiritual search... or my belief system.

See if you, too, can identify with James's side effects of over-enthusiastic spiritual seeking:

Evolving through making contact with the environment, objective reality? James wants to *evolve*, not get *involved*. So he struggles to find meaning.

Everything happens for a reason, right? Life itself can't be trusted, nor can his own instincts about making choices (supposedly). Instead, everyday life has become a puzzle where James' job is to figure out what he is *supposed* to do. Maybe his angels could tell him? Maybe a psychic?

Why care about that physical body? It's such a downer. If James could choose, he would banish forever that silly, boring body. Maybe he does the next best thing and neglects it. Or maybe James works really hard to perfect his body, eating only the purest of organic foods, doing yoga, etc. Either way, it's not much fun for James, having that body.

How about mindfulness, that very human Mecca? If James' spiritual path emphasizes mindfulness, he'll strive for it. Otherwise, he'll neglect it completely. Awareness with the mind is a very human enterprise, and James prefers godly, not human.

Having emotions, could that be worthwhile? Interpreting emotions seems so much more rewarding. James may have a habit of translating emotions as fast as they happen, bypassing direct feelings. Why not?

Depending on his belief system, James has the perfect label to define any emotion, explain it away or deal with it. Indeed, feeling emotions directly — without extra labeling — may be considered "unspiritual" or "un-evolved."

Is there a role for intellectual activity? James uses his intellect mostly to interpret experience in terms of his belief system. Maybe he belongs to a "Movement" that has taught him certain ways to speak about worldly things. Certainly, James prefers to bring any conversation around to his favorite topic, the spiritual.

Is this really as intellectually adventurous as it seems, or is it more like playing one favorite song again and again?

Loving that soul connection? Ironically, James is more at risk for neglecting his soul than someone who doesn't go spiritual. Why? He works so hard at what he is supposed to do. Living with soul means honoring human likes and dislikes, catching the spark that interests you and fanning it into a flame. James hardly trusts that.

YOUR ASSIGNMENT FOR DAY 18
If you are like James

What could help a big seeker like you to overcome deep resistance? Go back to Days 7-14. Do each of these chapters in turn, one day at a time, except skip Day 11, Spiritual Awareness Day. You've worked heroically hard at that part and, yes, you can be sure that God notices.

Why repeat the other chapters? It's not that last time you did them *wrong*. You're just becoming capable of doing them *better*. And here's the one thing I want you to do *differently* this time around: Gusto.

When you're enjoying your experience of body, etc., congratulate yourself. Say "Praise Jesus." (Substitute your favorite term for gusto.)

But then immerse yourself in the experience, as if human life really mattered. Remember, "This aspect of life is sacred or God never would have created it. It is spiritually safe for me to surrender to my human experience and enjoy it."

NO PROBLEM

Whew! You've read through three descriptions of deep resistance and can proudly say you don't have them. Excellent.

Also, give yourself credit for not making life all about your physical body. Even though some empaths have just one physical gift, Physical Intuition or Physical Oneness, I haven't yet encountered an empath who focuses only on physical life.

Why? My theory is that empaths, whatever their gifts, have been born too evolved to believe "I am my physical body."

Take your own survey. Ask any empath you know, "Do you believe that mainly you are your physical body?"

Anyway, you don't believe that, do you? You are an increasingly balanced combo of mind-body-spirit-intellect-soul-emotions-environment. And, therefore, you can progress from this page onward without having to repeat a single previous chapter.

YOUR ASSIGNMENT FOR DAY 18
If you haven't been stuck in any one category

You still could have deep resistance to fully living in the world as The Most Important Person in The Room. Let's find out how easy it is for you, doing today's assignment.

1. Add gusto. Continue being The Most Important Person in The Room and do it unapologetically, enthusiastically.
2. Continue to turn your gift(s) OFF whenever you notice that you have a choice. (And make it your business to notice when you have that choice.)
3. Use the "Take It" technique to keep other people's pain from sticking to you.
4. The Hello technique will continue to help you stay clear of other people's pain.
5. Finally, direct your consciousness, Being Deep, as needed to help you choose gusto.

Gusto is the basis of Empath Empowerment.

19. Pass the Test

Not to alarm you, but sometimes life is a test. For an empath, life poses certain exam questions daily. Answer them right and you become The Most Important Person in The Room. Answer them wrong and you suffer in ways that are all too familiar.

Day by day, you have been gaining skill at using your consciousness to ace that test. I'm very proud of you, Brave Explorer.

Underlying beliefs will keep you motivated (or not) to succeed completely with our 30-Day Plan, adding the rest of the skills needed for Empath Empowerment. Let's assess those relevant beliefs in today's Values Quiz.

VALUES QUIZ

Choose A or B to finish each statement.

1. What is good about being born as an empath:
A. Nothing. You're just meant to suffer.
B. Plenty. You have great opportunity to learn about people and help them.

2. The main benefit of being an empath is:
A. You can gain enormous wisdom while serving other people brilliantly.
B. Bragging rights are the point. Tell everybody you know who isn't an empath, "I'm more special."

3. How you can stop connecting to others super-deeply (just out of habit):

A. Cover up your problems with big, fake "boundaries" or an artificial "invisible shield." Or constantly analyze the STUFF you have taken on -- does it originally belong to yourself or to others?

B. Use skill to turn your gift(s) OFF. Then your gift(s) will be there, fresh and fine, to use whenever you do choose to turn the inner switch ON. As for STUFF belonging to others, it won't be there, period.

4. The key to using empath gift(s) safely is:

A. Develop the habit of keeping your gift(s) turned OFF as a matter of routine. To turn your gift(s) ON, use a safe technique. Otherwise, don't bother. Long term, your results won't be worth it.

B. Introduce yourself to people this way, "I'm Pat and I'm an empath. That means I'm weak and whiny, with a terrible psychic-level disability. Call Oprah! I'm ready to sob on the air, which could boost her ratings oh so much."

5. Is it okay to turn my empath gift(s) OFF most of the time?

A. No, since I have no right to take care of myself. Whenever I'm in the room with another person, that means I'm supposed to give. If I'm burned out, this is because of my fate.

B. Yes, of course I can turn my gift(s) OFF. I could even consider this an investment in helping others. Being rested and balanced as a person, I'll give better service whenever I do actively choose to turn my gift(s) ON. It's better to really help one person each day than to walk around tired and cranky, giving to everyone who crosses my path... and giving with only 2% clarity.

6. What does burnout mean to an empath?

A. Feeling burned out is a reminder to turn my gift(s) OFF. Hey, when people have problems, I am hardly the only empath or healer available.

B. Burnout represents wonderful proof of how special I am. Besides, paying attention to myself rather than others would make me selfish. To me, exhaustion means "Drink more coffee."

7. The very idea that I could aim my consciousness purposely as a skilled empath... brings up this reaction within me:

A. Hooray! I can do that. The main way to turn my gift(s) OFF is an occasional, super-easy tweak to my consciousness. There are so many categories: *MBS. I see!* Directing my consciousness can help me to access them all.

B. Sob, who me? Aim my consciousness? That wouldn't be fair. I have zero rights about doing things purposely. If other people could possibly benefit even slightly from my help, their needs trump mine. Obviously, everyone else in the universe is far more powerful, important, good looking, smells better, etc.

8. Guilt over turning my gift(s) OFF means that:

A. I am a good person and, possibly, saintly. The guiltier I feel, the more worthy am I.

B. Maybe I need some emotional or spiritual healing. Maybe I can do that healing on my own. Otherwise, if I need professional help, I'll make it my business to get some.

9. Other people I know don't yet have the kind of skills I am developing, and so:

A. Really, I ought to wait until everyone else is doing this Empath Empowerment thing before I fully commit. I'll use this book for light reading. Instead of using these 30 days to become a Skilled Empath, doing the daily assignments, I could make important investments in my popularity by collecting more friends at Facebook.

B. Who cares? If I don't advocate for my own happiness, nobody else will. Each person is responsible for his or her own life.

10. The worst thing that could happen if I turn OFF my gift(s) as an empath is:

A. My friends could die. I am the only savior.

B. I'll stop enabling people who have been stuck. Wait, that isn't so horrible — especially because everyone has access to God, everyone can choose to grow or not, and saving other adults has never been my responsibility at all.

11. Okay, the VERY worst thing that could happen if I turn my empath gift(s) off would be:

A. God will hate me and remove every bit of my sensitivity forever.
B. Nothing.

ANSWERS

Come on, you know which answers are correct. If you can't figure it
out on your own (and even if you can), try our next technique.

Inner Research

This inner research technique is a great way to get guidance
from within, guidance from your mind-body-spirit-intellect-
soul-emotions. The environment portion relates to wherever
you are doing the technique, sitting comfortably, paying attention to yourself.
Let's use Inner Research to experiment with the Values Quiz
you just did.

1. Close your eyes and notice how you feel.
2. Open your eyes. Choose any question you like from this
quiz. Read any answer provided. Repeat the memorable parts
in your head, thinking this slowly inside as if you were chew-
ing it with your mind.
3. Close your eyes. Take a couple of deep breaths. Notice how
you feel.
4. Open your eyes. Sort out the meaning of what you've experienced.

Your feelings count, whether they come from your physical
body, your emotions, your spirit... any category of who you
are. Every choice, viewed with Inner Research will bring forth
feelings. That information is valuable.
I trust you, and your sanity, for making the A or B choices in
line with becoming empowered as an empath.

What if some feelings surprise you? For instance, you research Question #6 and get to "Burnout represents wonderful proof of how spe-

cial I am." Theoretically, you know this answer is wrong. Yet perhaps part of you goes, "Ooh, but I really enjoy the martyrdom."

That information would be valuable. Don't deny any problems that pop up courtesy of our Values Quiz. Use your favorite resources for healing. You've got the power of your conscious mind, your subconscious mind, God, and about 10,000 top-notch healers of various kinds in the world who could help you, if asked.

Apart from helping you to make contact with any lingering problem that must be solved as part of your personal path to Skilled Empathdom, today you have learned a useful technique for making any choice. Inner Research Quickie takes one minute.

Inner Research Quickie

Now that you've experimented with Inner Research, use it on one real-life choice. This isn't a big psychic reading about the future. And you're not reaching for precognition about what effect your choice might have other people, simply researching yourself.

You know, The Most Important Person in The Room.

When deciding which choice to research, remember that every choice has at least two options. Research one option at a time.

For example: Ways you could tell your draining friend James that you cannot visit today.

Options could be:

• Lie, saying that you have an appointment.
• Say, "Before we plan our next visit, I need to talk about our relationship and work out some rules with you. There has been a pattern lately of your telling me your troubles for most of the visit.

"James, I'm really fond of you but I no longer wish to be available for that. Would you be willing to change that pattern? You know, we could talk about things other than your problems."

It's fascinating to spin out a consequence, doing Inner Research.

YOUR ASSIGNMENT FOR DAY 19

Let's continue your usual tactics to turn your gift(s) OFF:

- Research one more real life choice, doing Inner Research Quickie.
- Should problems of an objective nature come up in your life, do your best to solve them on the objective level. (The Magic Formula may do the trick, or maybe you'll need to figure out some other strategy.)
- Any time you're bored, play Advanced Bingo.
- Be Deep occasionally.
- And keep using Wakeup Call to keep yourself clear.

20. Hold a Space Like a Skilled Empath

Okay, you Kings and Queens of Skill-Directed Consciousness, you Mighty Majesties of The Room. Today is a great day indeed, greater than most days if you get it right. Because today you learn how a Skilled Empath holds a space.

I'm reasonably certain this will be way different from what you've been doing before.

What does it mean to hold a space? Whenever you pay attention to another person, you have a way to direct your consciousness. That way of holding a space can be changed, much as everyday habits with breathing can be changed, if you really want to experiment.

Unskilled empaths habitually hold a space differently from non-empaths. We get closer. Typically we whoosh in and out of the other person's auric field. Unless we know better, we don't call this "How I hold a space" but rather "Getting comfortable with another person" or even "Being normal."

Ha, normal for somebody who picks up pain!

Of course, you have habits for holding a space. You also have choices. Here's an analogy from the body language specialty called "proxemics." People from different cultures grow up learning to hold others at a certain physical distance. For instance, Italians stand closer than Germans.

Regardless of upbringing, however, you can consciously choose to change your habits with physical distance. Despite being of Italian descent, you can train yourself to stand closer, more like an German, or vice versa.

Similarly, you can change your comfort zone with inner space. This is really important for empaths.

HOLDING A SPACE

Holding a space means how close you get to a person by means of consciousness. This differs from merely paying attention.

You: Would you please pay attention while I'm talking to you?
Troy: I'm paying attention perfectly fine.
You: No way. You're texting. You're twittering. You're barely listening to me.
Troy: What, you want me to repeat back the very last things you said? I could.

Troy may pay attention just fine (by his standards) yet still not hold a space for you at all. (The technical term for this, as you will read soon, is "Space Dial Set at 1.")

Clues about paying attention show in body language, but this is completely separate from what's happening with consciousness. Jocelyn, in the same room with Troy and you, might seem completely disconnected from your conversation. Yet she could be intimately involved with both of you, doing Empath Merges galore.

You'd have to read auras to tell what was going on… or else doing a Skilled (not unskilled) Empath Merge.

No wonder far more people know about *paying attention* versus what happens with *holding a space*.

You, however, have developed the perfect background for exploring this. What prepared you? Some exercises on previous days, like Be Deep, actively used your consciousness. Today you will learn how to take that further, exercising a very subtle kind of muscle.

Normally, this muscle works all by itself but you can also move it on purpose, just like the fine muscles under your eyes.

Have you ever figured out how to round your eyes or narrow them? Then you can surely play with how you hold a space.

CONSCIOUSNESS MUSCLES

With the following exercise, don't mess around. Don't just read it. Do it. Otherwise, read the rest of this chapter later. For your first encounter, I want you to have the full-force, virginal, inner Aha!

For this introductory exercise, I'll use the term "Space Dial" but won't explain it much until you have had some direct, personal experience. Hey, you've already had 19 days to learn to trust me, so trust me on this.

EQUIPMENT

Preparing for this exercise, you will need one of the following, listed in order of best choice first:

1. A friend who is physically in the room with you, someone who agrees to be part of your experiment. He or she must also agree to do this exercise in silence, without giggling, complaining, texting, etc. (You only have the rest of your lives for all that.)

2. A photograph of someone you're fond of. This picture must show just this one person, taken from a front angle. The photo must also be large enough to show the person's face clearly.

3. A magazine or newspaper photo of a stranger, such as a fashion model. For our experiment to work, this photo must be from a front angle and be large enough to show the face clearly. Also, yes, by "person" I do mean somebody human. Cat gazing would be a different exercise.

POSITIONING

Next let's practice the physical part of Hold a Space. Let me play choreographer and you be the dancer. When I list the dance steps, don't trying to get into the mood of the dance. Just go through the motions, because we are practicing a technique, not doing it yet.

- With a person, sit opposite each other on chairs. From now on, I'll refer to this person as "your partner."
- Or, with a photo, sit comfortably. Hold up the photo so that you can see it on the level, as if it were a real person's face sitting across from yours. And yes, I'll refer to this "person" as "your partner."

Now, practice our Alternating Sequence, a kind of Peek a Boo for grownups:

1. Glance at one part of your partner's face (except avoid the eyes).
2. Then look away at something else in the room (like a wall).
3. Glance at one part of your partner's body (like one shoulder).
4. Look at something else in the room (like a chair).
5. Alternate looking at your partner and looking at something else in the room. Always avoid your partner's eyes.
6. Pace your looking to whatever speed you prefer, fast or slow. Only give equal time to both halves of the Alternating Sequence, seeing your partner and looking away.

Meet Your Space Dial

Your Space Dial is a faculty for holding a space. Now you've got all the basics for exploring it, so let's go for experience. Read through the following instructions, then *do* them step by step.

1. Close your eyes. Take a deep breath. Notice how it feels to be you right now. (Yes, this is like our earlier exercise to Be Deep.)
2. Then notice in a second way how it feels to be you. (Yes, this is like playing Advanced Bingo. Choose a different category of mind-body-spirit-intellect-soul-emotions-environment.)
3. Get Big. Think the name "God," or another name that you'd prefer as your highest source of inspiration right now. (One quick thought does it. You're connected.)
4. Set an intention with this quick thought, "I'm ready to learn more about myself."
5. Open your eyes. Do the Alternating Sequence for about two minutes.
6. Close your eyes. Take a deep breath. Notice how it feels to be you right now, checking in with both the categories you

explored before. Do you feel any different now? Ask this question in a simple, undemanding way.

7. Whether or not you notice any change is no big deal. Avoid using any interrogation techniques that might, or might not, be considered torture.

CONTROL OVER YOUR SPACE DIAL

This alternating sequence was practice for the skill I'll help you learn next. Hint: It's about gaining control over your Space Dial. In the past you have developed habits for holding a space with another person. Probably you don't appreciate yet just how high you turn that Space Dial. You barely know that you have such a thing as a Space Dial!

Here's some perspective. For years, I've been researching how different people hold a space. My research method involves doing Empath Merges on a wide variety of people, using techniques like the one you'll learn on Day 28.

Having conducted hundreds of these experiments in consciousness, I'm convinced that empaths and non-empaths have radically different ways of holding a space.

Unskilled empaths hold a space with great intimacy. Compared to that – I'll be blunt here — non-empaths hold a space where other people are treated more like objects. (This kind of reality is equally valuable for human evolution, just different from what we empaths instinctively do.)

What does it mean to experience somebody like an object? Surely you've seen it happen:

- Say that you go to a speed-dating event where singles are being looked up and down, scrutinized like food at the meat market. Should *you* walk in there with a super-buff body, suitably groomed and dressed, you will be treated as a "sex object."
- Imagine a family reunion, where you're part of a large family. Out of the whole bunch, you happen to be the one person who has managed to become rich. To your family, you may no longer seem like a person. Instead, you're

someone to ask for a loan. Or a gift. Or a large inheritance. Goodbye person, hello "money object."

- In another example, you're in college. It's easy for you, with your genius I.Q. and excellent study habits.
Congratulations! Except some kids make friends with you for ulterior motives. They don't want your company so much as free tutoring. In short, to them, you have become a "brain object."

These are extreme examples. But in everyday life, non-empaths view all people more or less as objects, as illustrated by the drawing opposite.

Imagine that every human being has a built-in Space Dial. Non-empaths naturally have this dial set at 1. Empaths naturally set it at 10. Consider this a default position, a habit.

Keeping your Space Dial at 1 means that other people seem like objects. Only a narcissist has no desire to ever turn that Space Dial higher. Non-empaths prize moving it higher. But how much higher?

- A non-empath trying to get close to another person might go up to a 3.
- A non-empath who falls in love will spontaneously move that Space Dial up to a 4.
- Taking care of one's baby, a non-empath might move that Space Dial as far as a 4.
- A non-empath having sex might manage a temporary turn-on of that Space Dial all the way up to 5. Then, wham, bam! It's back to 1.

Maybe that's why pop culture makes such a big deal of sex. Generations ago, people used to say of great sex, "The earth moved for me."

Then and now, sex just might represent a non-empath's best chance to move beyond having consciousness centered in his or her physical body.

Honestly, as an empath, you may have had great sex. Hope so! But did you ever feel that sex was the *only* time you moved far away from feeling centered in your physical body?

Space Dial Fully ON

Compare that to life as a non-empath, so unaware of your inner consciousness that you could mistake when *you* move into a depth experience of your lover with having *the earth* around you move?

Back when you did the previous exercise, you weren't asked to have sex. I didn't even ask you to adjust your Space Dial. So you had it set at your usual default position... probably at 10.

Now let's get some contrast going. Soon I'll ask you to do the Alternating Sequence again with just one difference.

This time, when you alternate with your partner, look at your partner as if he/she were just another piece of furniture.

YES, FURNITURE

Practice this furniture idea before we go fully into doing the technique.

- Move your eyes around the room where you are.
- Look, then move. Look, then move.
- Don't linger too long on any one object. A brisk pace will help you remain on the surface.

Notice? You do have a way of looking at furniture! It doesn't walk or talk or breathe (unless it's a very expensive piece of furniture). So, empath or not, you know how to treat furniture as an inanimate object.

In our next technique, your assignment is to treat your partner just the same way. Meat at the singles event! A brain in the genius-at-school fantasy! I call this variation on our Space Dial exercise "The Furniture Game." Weird though it may feel, do it anyway.

The Furniture Game

1. Position yourself with "your partner" opposite, both of you sitting comfortably. (That partner could be a willing human volunteer or a photograph.)

2. Close your eyes. Take a deep breath. Notice how it feels to be you right now.

3. Then notice in a second way how it feels to be you. (Choose a different category of mind-body-spirit-intellect-soul-emotions-environment.)

4. Get Big. Think the name "God," or another name that you'd prefer to call on your highest source of inspiration. (One quick thought does it. You're connected.)

5. Set an intention with this quick thought, "I'm ready to learn more about myself."

6. Open your eyes. Do the Alternating Sequence for about two minutes. In this version, you will treat your partner like furniture.

7. Close your eyes. Take a deep breath. How does it feel to be you right now? Notice your first category chosen before, then

> your second category. Has anything about your inner experience shifted?

DID THE EARTH MOVE FOR YOU?

Put those clothes back on!

Seriously, now that you've played The Furniture Game, how was it different from when you did The Basic Space Dial Exercise?

In particular, did you change as much? Think again about the comparison, being aware of yourself at the start vs. the end.

In my workshops, most students notice a big difference immediately. With their Space Dials naturally turned up to 10, they tend to pick up STUFF belonging to their partner. With their Space Dials turned down to 1, they don't. Can you relate?

If we were in a workshop together, by now one of you would be raising your hand to complain:

"I may have felt better, but it scared me, turning my Space Dial down to 1."

How about you? Did you fear one these side effects?

- The other person might notice.
- The other person might think you are selfish.
- The other person might die from lack of attention.

Actually, none of this happens, especially that death part. Remember, most people are non-empaths. And since they keep their Space Dials at 1 most of the time, when you go from 10 to 1, how would they know the difference?

You can safely adapt The Furniture Game to different social situations, whether it's hanging out with your roommate or discretely watching strangers on a bus. This technique is meant to be used with eyes open. Just avoid doing it while multi-tasking.

Why no multi-tasking? Unless you can give this technique your full attention for 1-2 minutes, you're better off not doing it. Multi-tasking would dilute the effectiveness of the technique and could even spoil it for use in the future.

Space Dial Fully OFF

So let that roommate talk but don't try talking yourself. Sitting on that bus, do a Space Dial Shift as a passenger, not as the driver.

Space Dial Shifts in Everyday Life

As with any of the techniques in this 30-Day Plan, don't even chew gum as you go through the steps of technique. No dividing your mind!

1. Start noticing how you are using your consciousness right now. Notice in two different ways, just as you did when playing The Furniture Game, except that now your eyes are open. Choose from mind-body-spirit-intellect-soul-emotions-environment.

2. Ask yourself, "How have I been using my Space Dial just now?"

3. Set the intention to turn your Space Dial to the number of your choice. It could be 1, 4, 7 or any other number you choose. After all, that Space Dial does belong to you. Just one quick thought inside is enough of an intention, such as "I'm turning my Space Dial to 4 now."

4. Once you have set that intention, your consciousness will follow. Trust that.

5. For the next few seconds, move your eyes in the same pattern as with The Furniture Game, alternating between a real live person vs. furniture.

6. You've got the flow going. Excellent!

7. Notice how it feels to be you. Check this out in a couple of ways, the same ones you used before.

8. Consider this information for a moment. It's valuable information about what it's like for you, with your Space Dial set at the number you've chosen.

Resume your same intention as at Step 3. Continue, doing the occasional inner reminding about intention. Or do a quick bit of Furniture Game.

Playing with this new technique, explore one Space Dial setting at a time. Practice doing one number at a time. Soon you'll have a working definition for each Space Dial setting from 1-10.

Just don't try to be precise, like an engineer. Be sloppy!

Learning about your Space Dial is like learning to ride your first ten speed bike. As you get the hang of your machine, you develop an instinct for which gear to use.

Because you're an empath, not a bicycle, a lower setting on your Speed Dial isn't just for slow speeds or going uphill. Space Dial at 1 will emphasize you.

Beware the "comfort" that really is habit, where it feels "so natural" to emphasize the other person with your consciousness, even if you wind up feeling pretty bad afterwards.

During our 30-Day Plan, whenever you have a choice, aim for being The Most Important Person in The Room. You'll take on less STUFF. Or none. Space Dial at 1 can become second nature, your default position.

AVOIDING EYES

Here comes some extra help for keeping your Space Dial set to 1. Avoid direct eye contact with other people. When a person makes eye contact with someone else, both of their Space Dials usually zoom right up to the highest setting available. Only for a non-empath it's 3, whereas you tend to go up to 10.

In real life, how can you get around eye contact if another person expects it of you? For the next few days, experiment with Eye Option #1.

Eye Option #1

To protect yourself from involuntarily turning that Space Dial up, look in the eye *area*, rather than directly at another person's eyes.

If you look at Lexi's forehead, one of her eyebrows or one of her ears, she won't know the difference. Most people won't.

By using Eye Option #1 exclusively for 3-5 days, you will strengthen your core sense of self. Then you'll be ready for Eye Option #2, a second alternative to staring deeply at eyes.

Eye Option #2

In a social situation where eye contact seems required, take only a super-quick glance at the other person's eyes. That would be one second or less.

Immediately move your eyes in a different direction.

Why the big rush, just one second? Say that it's summer and your feet are bare. Until now, you have been standing on a nice, cool lawn. But now you must quickly walk down a bit of pavement. Man, but that's hot! So you walk really fast. Do the same thing now, only with eyeballs. Skitter across that slightly dangerous territory.

When you stare eye-to-eye for two seconds or more, you won't risk burning your body. But you will risk turning your Space Dial up to 10, out of habit.

Don't. One second is plenty to make sure that Lexi still has two eyes, they're not rolled up in her head, etc.

Losing your customary, automatic way of eye-gazing will be your big gain as a person. Maybe you're skeptical, but you're on a 30-Day Plan, not a lifetime sentence. Find out what this experiment can do for you. It just might improve your life in ways you can't yet imagine.

YOUR ASSIGNMENT FOR DAY 20

Today is such an important day in your development as a Skilled Empath. When was the last day you discovered a new body part? Was it back when you were an infant, lying on your back and giggling uncontrollably as you played with your toes?

Like a part of your body, that Space Dial is a subtle faculty within your consciousness. Here's how to profit from this tremendously important new discovery:

1. Keep your Space Down at 1 most of the time. (Do the technique for Space Dial Shifts in Everyday Life. If extra oomph is needed, give yourself a round of The Furniture Game.)
2. If you're really itching to turn up your Space Dial a few times today, don't go higher than 4.
3. Avoid looking people in the eye. Use Eye Option #1. Look at nearby parts of the face, rather than at the eyes themselves.
4. The rest of today, see if you can have a couple of interactions with a real-live person. Non-technological, non-twittering, not with cell — eek! Yes, it is possible. You could do some no-tech visiting, talking, touching, sharing meals, etc.

5. While you do this, experiment with keeping that Space Dial at 1. Notice how, both during and after each interaction, you can feel like The Most Important Person in The Room. Others are unlikely to notice, but you'll feel the difference.

AMBITIOUS?

Okay, I can't resist. Here's one optional assignment, in case you're really, really ambitious. Say that you want to become a Skilled Empath as quickly as possible.

Doing Eye Option #1, you may feel rebellious. It could happen that sometimes you won't want to break that old stare habit. When this happens, take a deep breath and ask inside, "What's bothering me?"

Whatever answer you get, whether or not it makes a whole lot of sense, *write it down.*

Throughout the day, make a running list.

Don't worry about interpreting that list. Just have it handy when you join me for tomorrow, Day 21.

Day 21. Redefine Your Job

Step right up, folks. Today you get to grieve. Well, maybe it will turn out more like nostalgia or guilt or laughing your head off at the foolishness of the past.

Why? I'm going to help you gain extra skill at using your Space Dial. Yesterday, of course, was the Super-Duper, Inner High-Tech Day when you officially learned how to treat other people like furniture. I raised the shocking idea that non-empaths do this most of the time.

Even more shocking, you began actually *doing* The Furniture Game — I hope — which probably felt weird but strangely good.

If you followed through on your homework, you kept your Space Dial set at 1 for most of the day. So *a reaction* has probably set in, either grief or guilt or whatever.

Of course, your main reaction could have been positive. Did you notice subtle life-affirming emotions like more self-confidence or greater self-compassion? (These are definitely going to be your long-term benefits from keeping that Space Dial at 1.)

Unfortunately, you may not be used to paying attention to subtle life-affirming emotions, despite being very, very familiar with feelings like guilt.

So let's dedicate today to rehab. If you did the optional homework from yesterday, take out your list about old space-holding habits. Read it over. Which buttons did it push for you, turning down that Space Dial?

Consider everything you wrote as information about being stuck... in an old habit that didn't serve you. You're still learning as an empath, though more skilled than before. It's Day 21 of our 30-Day Plan, compared to years when you lived with the equivalent of zero potty training. Apart from habit, there's no good reason to keep your Space Dial at 10, not if you want to serve humanity and gain wisdom as a Skilled Empath.

POSITIVE CHANGE

Now hear this, whether or not you consciously noticed a lot of discomfort yesterday. Turning your empath gift(s) OFF means more than removing something, like turning your Space Dial down to a lower number.

Should it count as a loss, going from a big, heroic, self-sacrificing 10 to a puny 1? I think not. Whenever you turn that Space Dial *down,* you're turning *up* something else.

Automatically you turn the mighty power of your consciousness toward yourself. Fascinating though you have been before, you'll become way more fascinating to yourself.

And, yes, this fascination may even turn contagious. Think of it like measles, only better looking. When you experience yourself as interesting — not just liking the idea, but living it —other people will find you more interesting, too.

For sure, Brave Explorer, turning *down* that Space Dial means that something else automatically turns *up.* You become The Most Important Person in The Room, which means that you are more than a…

BUT, BUT, BUT

I'm not here to dictate what you must believe. Last time I checked, even God didn't do that. But, but, but I do want to encourage you to use freedom of choice about what you believe. You could, for instance, choose to *believe in yourself as someone important.*

Certain popular beliefs in society are especially damaging to empaths. They acknowledge that "I do have value as a person" but, but, but …

- Men (or women) are like babies. For my love relationship to work, I must anticipate what my mate needs, then deliver it.
- Love means giving so much that it hurts.

- In order to be a good Christian (or devout follower of any religion), I must constantly sacrifice my own happiness.
- For my love life to work, I must maintain constant maximum-depth connection. Otherwise how will I know where I stand?
- It's my job to give like crazy whenever at work. After all, I'm a nurse, therapist, taxi driver, inmate escort at a prison, etc. (Fill in the blank with ANY profession.)
- When I was a child growing up with that alcoholic parent, Pat, I had to anticipate whatever Pat would do next; it was a matter of survival. Now, even though I'm no longer living in that dysfunctional family, I still feel I'll be safer if I keep all my empath circuits turned ON.

Why would such dismal beliefs serve you now? Maybe you find this short list of buts way too extreme. Yet you still feel guilty over turning down your Space Dial. Maybe you have a fine civilized *but*, a small tasteful *but*... as it were. Which words, exactly, are inscribed on your *but*?

Ask yourself, for pity's sake. And then ask yourself, "Why would this be true for me NOW?"

You can use your freedom of belief to provide some much needed wiggle room and, eventually, a good life besides. For instance, going back over our previous short list, you could change the self-talk.

- Sure, some men (and women) are like babies. But you don't have to choose a person like that to live with and be your love. Instead, you could choose a mate whose emotional age is older than two.
- Definitely, love means giving so hard that it hurts... if you're dating the Marquis de Sade. If a demanding sadist is your idea of a desirable companion, you really ought to get out more.
- In order to be a good Christian, etc. you must what? Please! Pull out your Bible or Book of Mormon or Upanishads or whatever and find me the quote. Is that grotesque suffering

thing really, truly, required by your religion? If ever you were taught such a thing, question the source.

Wasn't it a dysfunctional or power-hungry practitioner of your religion? Maybe someone well meaning and maybe not!

For every suffering saint you know, there are plenty of psychologically healthy members of that very same religion. They help others at least as much as the suffering sort. Plus they have way more fun.

- Speaking of fun, what's the payoff for you to stay in a relationship where you must keep yourself so terribly vigilant? Is this relationship spelled L*O*V*E or S*C*A*R*Y?

- As an empath, you may have assumed it's your job to give like crazy at work. But take a new look at people you meet who also work as nurses, therapists, escorts at your nearest prison, etc.

  Most are not empaths. If professionally trained, they were taught a skill set based on *not* being empaths. Yes, that is true even of nurses, psychotherapists, etc.

  You, too, can use *only* that professional skill set at work, keeping your gift(s) turned OFF. Not only can you do that. It could even land you a raise. (See Gordon's story, coming soon.)

- How about surviving childhood abuse, alcoholic parents, dysfunctional families, etc.? I see a lot of this pain second-hand as a healer, because I help clients to release the STUFF they're still carrying from hellish childhoods, usually by cutting cords of attachment.

Healing STUFF from your aura might be a really smart idea. Yet one more reason to do this: You'll find it easier to learn the skills of Empath Empowerment.

HOW NON-EMPATHS COPE

What will it mean, long term, to develop the habit of living with Space Dial at 1? Among my students, a new fear often comes up around this stage in Empath Empowerment. It's the fear that if your Space Dial won't bring you big knowledge about everyone you meet, automatically you will become completely clueless.

Fear not. Becoming a Skilled Empath doesn't mean having your perceptiveness downgraded to the level of a charcoal briquette. Allow me to introduce you to a very fine technique you can use for getting information. Non-empaths use it and so can you.

All caring people want to gather information about the folks they care about. The urge to know can feel like an itch. In the past, as a not-yet-skilled empath, you would deal with this itch by using your gift(s). This was the equivalent of shooting an ant with a cannon, but what did you know? Probably you didn't even know that you were an empath in the first place.

So you would satisfy human curiosity by doing a quick, unskilled and unconscious Empath Merge. Or maybe you would do a slow, longish but still sadly unskilled, Empath Merge.

Give yourself a shout-out for being mega-talented. To you, doing that movement with consciousness was no big deal. Non-empaths don't have that option.

Yet somehow they do manage to satisfy their human itch for information. They know about a technique that you have probably used on occasion, too: Asking Human Questions.

Asking Human Questions

The advantage to you of using this technique is that *you can actually substitute it for doing an Empath Merge.*

1. When you feel that familiar itch to get more information about somebody, create a question.
2. Phrase it in plain, old everyday human language. This doesn't have to be highly sophisticated. Just make it a real question, rather than a generic, like "How ya doing?"
3. The simple act of finding a question can help you to calm down and not feel as though you must use your empath superpowers.

Here are examples of questions that you might uncover through this technique:

- After that 12-course banquet I just served you, are you still hungry?
- Are you mad at me or just perpetually cranky?
- Have I groveled enough for today?

Okay, maybe you won't use exactly these words. Not out loud. Not directly to your significant other.

Merely deciding which questions you'd like to ask — Aha! That can bring you plenty of answers. What *do* you really want to know? Hmmmm.

It's perfectly safe to ask any question out loud… when alone in the bathroom. Before you trot out that question to your significant other, double check. Is that question really such a prize pony? Might it be more like a wounded cockroach?

Besides, your question may have a simple answer that you can figure out all by yourself, such as:

- Calm down.
- Take a deep breath.
- I'm okay.

Or maybe you'll choose to rephrase your question by using The Magic Formula, which you learned back on Day 17.

Sometimes becoming a Skilled Empath brings up issues and tissues. If this happens, you don't have to hide it from your significant other. By now you're on Day 21 of a 30-Day Plan. Which you're not required to keep a secret.

Depending on the amount of suffering in your past, you may feel delicate about developing the social skill called "Asking Human Questions." Maybe you're worried about putting your S.O. on the defensive. Then you can preface your questions. Examples follow.

- This is my fear, okay. But are you angry at me for breathing through my nose?
- I've been worrying. When I do the laundry and our towels

come out of the dryer only two-inches fluffy-soft, do you despise me as a person?

- This may be a silly question. But when you come home, you never fold me in a big bear hug and tickle my toes. Of course, everybody knows that if you really, truly love someone, you do that daily. So I'm wondering, why haven't you ever tickled my toes?

Alas, there's a finite limit to how many questions like these I can supply for you. You're going to have to find the most important, most personal ones on your own. Likewise, if you have resistance keeping your Space Dial at 1 in everyday life, only one person can find the solution, a person you know rather intimately.

But here is one way I can help: Providing success stories. The following tales come from students who overcame their resistance to keeping their Space Dials at 1. Maybe their stories will inspire you.

JUANITA'S FRIENDLY SKIES

When Juanita worked as a flight attendant, she attracted all the crazies. Mysterious but true....

There she would be, standing with her fellow crew members at the entrance to the plane, welcoming passengers. At first glance, Juanita could tell who would be trouble. Sure enough, during the flight they would ask for her, never the other flight attendants. The entire flight, troubled travelers would spill their sob stories, their insecurities, their multiple cocktails.

Nutty passengers would get out of their seats, walk down the aisles of the plane, and target Juanita. Then they would supply way too much information about their lives.

Juanita began to wonder if, unintentionally, she wore some kind of wacko-magnet on her airline uniform.

Actually she did. Only it showed on the level of her aura. This magnet read "Space Dial turned up to 10. Ladies and gentlemen, get your free unskilled Empath Merge. Hurry, hurry, step right up. Dump your STUFF right here."

In practical terms, Juanita's aura wasn't terribly different from these famous words:

Give me your tired, your poor,
Your huddled masses yearning to breathe free,

The wretched refuse of your teeming shore.
Send these, the homeless, tempest-tost to me.

This is a great offer. Especially when it's free. But this offer is appropriate for the Statue of Liberty, not a person made of flesh and blood.

Eventually Juanita decided to try an experiment. She would turn her Space Dial down to 1 and do everything in her job description, nothing more and, especially, no more volunteering energetic support to every passenger on the plane. Instead, Juanita decided, her goals would be having a pleasant, easy flight (Priority #1) and doing her job (Priority #2).

In short, she'd just go through the motions.

Woweee! Crazies started heckling the other flight attendants. Crazies left Juanita alone. She kept her job, too.

Feeling better as a Skilled Empath, Juanita still helped people plenty. Only now she did it when she decided to do so, not because needy people happened to be in the vicinity.

It's true. Space Dial at 10 is never, ever in your job description. Don't confuse volunteer work with a 9-5 job. And, speaking of jobs....

GORDON'S PERFORMANCE EVALUATION

Gordon had a problem with his boss. Mr. Boss was always telling Gordon, "You're too much." Yet Gordon had no clue what he was doing wrong, or what he could do about it.

From the way he described his work life to me, Gordon was an exemplary employee. Yet he also happened to be an immensely talented unskilled empath, with circuits wide open.

After studying with me, Gordon developed control over turning his gifts OFF. Returning to work, he followed my recommendations, keeping his Space Dial at 1 whenever he dealt with Mr. Boss.

Soon Mr. Boss was telling him, "I don't know why but lately I've started feeling more comfortable with you."

Mr. Boss started taking Gordon out to lunch. Instead of being fired, Gordon received a promotion.

What made the difference? When you keep your empath gift(s) ON constantly, the recipient of your attention will notice. In a way.

Mr. Boss doesn't have to be an empath in order to tell that something is happening on the level of consciousness. It can be just a vague feeling.

Mr. Boss may never tell you his reaction in words. Consciously he may never notice a thing. Nonetheless, he'll react subconsciously to being the object of your unskilled Empath Merges. Maybe he'll like the attention but maybe he won't. In that case, he may develop conscious thoughts like these:

- Gordon is smothering me. He reminds me of my mother.
- When I'm with Gordon, I feel like he knows my secrets.
- There's something weird/obnoxious/not-quite-right about Gordon.

Yes, I know this seems unfair and ungrateful. But not everybody wants to be helped.

A reaction like Mr. Boss' is not about how great you are. Really, how sweet that (until quite recently) whenever you've been in the room with other people, you have lifted pain and fear out of their auras! However, some people actually prefer keeping their STUFF.

- Subconsciously, they notice when it is gone and will replace it as soon as possible.
- Ironically, they will blame you for making them feel uncomfortable.

Bizarre though this sounds, remember that everyone in this world is not identical to you. Compared to you, some are slow growers. In fact, some don't want to grow at all.

Personally, I went through decades without understanding this. I worked heroically hard to interest everyone I met in "evolving." (And, of course, that meant "evolving according to my beliefs.")

This did not make me popular. It made me obnoxious.

Everyone here at Earth School has the right to choose the curriculum. People are allowed to grow quickly or slowly, depending on their sacred use of free will.

Certainly a Mr. Boss in your life *who wants your help* is capable of letting you know. Remember, he can use his words, too.

YOUR ASSIGNMENT FOR DAY 21

Brave Explorer, here's your job for today:

1. If you want to learn more about people, use your words, not your empath gift(s). When you have questions, try Asking Human Questions rather than relying on your familiar method of finding answers through unskilled Empath Merge.

2. Lavish attention on the objective side of relationships, rather than your subjective commentaries. (Ironically, this may make you *more* popular.)

3. After you turn your gift(s) OFF, what if you start feeling guilt or some other discomfort? Notice that. Then repeat this helpful phrase, "So what?" Emphasize whatever else is interesting as you go your merry way being The Most Important Person in the Room.

What will you choose to do about that silly old Space Dial habit? You could blame an ungrateful world. But, but, but maybe you'll choose something easier. You could simply redefine your job.

Day 22. New Eyes

Thanks to The Furniture Game and Asking Human Questions, you're gaining control over how you hold a space with others. Yesterday should have helped, too. But maybe you're grumbling like Jocelyn, who still is fixated on eyes:

"Sorry, Rose, but I've simply got to look everyone in the eye. Otherwise, I feel inauthentic. Turning off empath gifts is fine. But where's the fun in life if you can't look at people's eyes all you want?"

Gee, would I be capable of understanding that? As a lovelorn teenager, I taped just one crush-worthy picture on my bedroom walls. Actually, I placed it on the ceiling, right above my bed. It was two pages from an art book, two super-enlarged photographs of Pablo Picasso's eyes. One page per eye. My centerfold.

Yes, I kept those humungous eyes above my bed so I could stare at them meaningfully. This brought such improvement to my hours of insomnia.

Jocelyn, and everyone else, I know better than to demand that you permanently forego looking at eyes all you want. I'm only warning you: If you were born as an empath, no matter which gift(s) you have, guess what happens as soon as you look directly at any live person's eyes for two seconds straight?

Your consciousness starts to travel into that person's aura. If you are not a very, extremely, hugely accomplished Skilled Empath, you'll do a quick unskilled Empath Merge and take some of that person's STUFF directly into your aura.

The exceptions would be if you're watching a photo or screen image. Or you're staring at your *own* eyes for two seconds or more for a practical purpose, such as inserting contact lenses or applying eye makeup. In this case, you're treating yourself like furniture, right?

During our 30 Days, you're experimenting, and with something far more interesting than plum-colored eyeliner. I'm helping you to land squarely into your own life, saving Empath Merges for special occasions.

My purpose isn't to deprive you of adventure but to help you to discover one great big adventure: Being yourself, through and through, whether with friends or not, always and consistently remaining The Most Important Person in The Room.

Come to think of it, haven't you started to feel differently about yourself since your Day 1 with this book? Yes? No? Either way, here's a fun idea.

SKILL SNEAKING UP ON ME

It's quiz time, Brave Explorer. Answer YES, NO or MAYBE to each of the following questions.

1. I *am* becoming more aware of myself, my full set of mind-body-spirit-intellect-soul-emotions-environment.

2. I have started to have fun with these different aspects of myself, choosing to jump into different categories rather than mostly staying stuck at one level.

3. At least once during the last three days, I have purposely pulled awareness away from emotions or intellect or spirit, thinking something like, "There can be more to my life than this." Then I have chosen to direct my consciousness elsewhere, to another part of my personal Bingo card... and it worked.

4. When I'm in the room with other people, I have been paying more attention to myself than before.

5. God hasn't struck me dead for doing this, either. In fact, nobody has been injured by the subtle, personal choice to shift my consciousness back to myself.

6. I'm actually beginning to grow comfortable with the idea of treating myself like The Most Important Person in The Room. It has stopped seeming so selfish and started feeling perfectly reasonable.

7. I have noticed that other people in my life, the non-empaths, really do have their Space Dials turned down to 1 most of the time. This doesn't make them monsters. They're just very focused on their own lives.

8. Also, I've started noticing how some people (especially empaths) stick to other people like glue. There's a possible smothering effect on the person being stuck to. In the past, I didn't notice this, but now I do: *The recipient of an unskilled empath's attention doesn't necessarily like it.*

9. My anxiety level has gone way down, come to think of it.

10. Subtly, it has become easier to keep my mind on work. I'm getting more accomplished, just being me without adding all that volunteer work.

11. Although I continue to use The Wakeup Call as needed to clear out STUFF from others, I'm not having to do it as often. Could I be clearer than before? Could I get used to feeling more powerful, more like myself?

For every YES answer, congratulate yourself. MAYBE's aren't bad, either. You're becoming a Skilled Empath at your own pace, that's all.

WHO OWNS THOSE EYES, ANYWAY?

One way to pick unskilled empaths out of a crowd is to watch how they use their eyes. Many unskilled empaths stare like babies. (The exception to this rule is the mating behavior of non-empaths and empaths alike. When love-struck, all people do an awful lot of staring.)

Before you began our 30-Day Plan, didn't you tend to stare at people, especially looking them straight in the eye? Would you like to have *more* (not *fewer*) ways of using your eyes, and do it risk free? Today we're going to explore new techniques that, besides being fun, will add to your skill as an empath.

In the past you had just one major choice about how you used your eyes in social situations. Would you stare, yes or no? But you've already learned some useful alternatives:

- With The Furniture Game, you explored a new choice that combined intention ("like furniture") with the use of your own personal eyeballs.
- With Eye Option #1, you stopped automatically making eye contact for social reasons. Instead, you experimented with looking *near* eyes, not *at* them.
- With Eye Option #2, you were invited to experiment by taking only a *quick glance,* one second or less, rather than jumping in for a prolonged stare.

Thus, you have started to gain control over how you use your eyes. Which leaves you feeling better than before. Which is the point.

What, have some of you been cheating?

'Fess up, have you been doing all the other techniques in our 30-Day Plan, just not this one? So you didn't want to make the sacrifice! Well, that's akin to a dieter who eats sensibly all day long except, at night, he or she absolutely must devour that big carton of ice cream.

If you have been cheating with your eyes, think about this: Who do those eyes belong to, anyway? Maybe somebody else expects you to stare, siphoning off huge amounts of your own psychic energy and dumping his/her STUFF into you. To use a technical term, "Phooey on that-ey."

If Roscoe needs that kind of help, trust me. He'll be able to find it. You're not the only empath with eyeballs. In America, 1 out of 20 people is an empath and most of them probably do have eyeballs.

Let somebody else volunteer. In the unlikely event that Roscoe can't find another unskilled empath, maybe he'll hit bottom and start taking responsibility for solving his own problems.

Managing the use of your eyeballs, you can be like a doctor who takes the Hippocratic Oath. From now on, do no harm, not to people like Roscoe (by enabling them) and not to yourself, either.

You can actually use your eyes to make yourself The Most Important Person in The Room. There's a whole set of techniques for this. I call them "Eye Muscles."

Unlike my old Picasso eyes on the ceiling, live people have muscles for moving their eyes. Although eyes can move quite nicely with *involuntary* muscles, eyes can also be moved by means of *voluntary* muscles. It's like breathing, which normally goes by itself. But you might consciously change how you breathe for yoga or acting or singing or spitting.

Voluntary control of your eyes is essential for Empath Empowerment. Yet unskilled empaths seldom take control. Instead, they indulge in a trusting kind of stare that brings on unskilled Empath Merge.

Say that James, still an unskilled empath, is in a room when Lexi enters. All the time they're together, James looks at her as if she's the star of his movie.

Poor besotted James. (You already know about his hopeless crush, right?) Often James makes matters worse for himself by prolonged staring at Lexi's eyes. Whenever James does this, his consciousness does super-fast unskilled Empath Merges with Lexi, taking on more of her STUFF. Which could help explain why, at the end of the day, James feels as though he belongs in a recycle bin.

Yech!

Eye Muscles

Be the star of your own movie. Decide how far to move out with your eyes. Those eyes do belong to you, correct?
Here is a set of five advanced eye techniques. Used them alone or in combination, as you wish.

1. Look in the *very near distance*. Move your vision out just a little, eyes angled downward, aiming very close to you, only a few feet ahead.

2. Look out *mid-range.* You're moving eyes farther away this time. Don't aim really far from you but at a comfortable middle distance.

3. Look *very far out* now, as if aiming for the horizon. To do this, move your eyes so the gaze lifts upward.

4. Activate your *sideways* eye muscles. Slowly alternate moving your eyes to the left, then the right. Moving sideways, you can choose whether to look mid-range or up close. You might even notice objects with your peripheral vision, out the corner of one eye. Are your eyes clever or what?

5. When you're in the room with somebody else, choose not to focus constantly on that person. Who are you going to make The Most Important Person in The Room? It's you, with those fine eye muscles. So alternate:

- Sometimes looking at other people
- Sometimes looking elsewhere

That's right. No longer must you automatically focus 100% on other people in the room. Your eyes obey YOU.

But are these eye tricks socially acceptable? Sure, provided you don't dart your eyes around super-fast or roll them around like pinwheels.

Every time you make a voluntary shift to eye position, you're using your own consciousness to control which person in the room becomes the most important to you.

Aim your eyes purposely and the very act of choosing makes you The Most Important Person in The Room.

Incidentally, if you're shy about trying out this new eye behavior in front of people you know, practice while watching TV. Drag your eyes away from the actor who is speaking lines and notice how other actors react. Or check out the furniture, on-screen or off-screen.

Will the show still go on? Find out.

HYPNOSIS ALERT

Hypnotists aren't the only ones who put people into trances. People put themselves into trances. James, for instance, puts himself into a trance by staring at Lexi.

Being an unskilled empath means often putting yourself into an unskilled empath's trance, one where you (Sob!) *never* get to be The Most Important Person in The Room.

It's human to identify with others. Most people do it most of the time. But if you're an empath, you don't simply identify with somebody like Lexi. Your empath gift(s) turn ON and, before you know it, that Space Dial twirls up to a 10.

Letting this happen is optional for you now. This skill comes none too soon, because every unskilled empath trance brings consequences. And these may not be terribly good for you. Here are three example of unskilled Empath Merge being seriously dangerous.

BRAD'S TRANCE OF MISERY

Once I gave a workshop where the graduate, Brad, told this story:

"I began noticing the problem in second grade. Pain from the other kids would come into me and I didn't know how to stop it. Now I know I am an empath with the gift of Physical Oneness.

"Before I just knew that I would develop health problems. In the past, I was hospitalized 12 times because of different health problems that really came from other people. I knew what was happening, only I was powerless to stop it.

"Studying with you has been the first time I can remember when I could be in a room with other people and pay attention to myself."

Maxi, another student in that workshop, told her story of life in an unskilled empath's trance.

MUSICAL CHAIRS WITH MAXI

"Now I know that I have Emotional Oneness, Emotional Intuition, Spiritual Oneness, Spiritual Intuition, and Physical Oneness. Before, I knew only this: Whenever I was with other people, I would take on their anger, their worries and even their aches and pains.

"Whenever I would ride the subway, sitting next to a stranger, I would take on her problems. After I couldn't stand it any more, I would change seats. Sometimes I would use up every seat in that subway car. Then I would have to move to another subway car and start changing seats all over again.

"That's how it was until yesterday, Day One of our workshop. But when I came here today for Day Two of our workshop, I didn't have to change seats once. I just realized that now."

Towanda, another woman in that same workshop, decided to tell her story, too.

TOWANDA'S TRANSPORT

"I used to change seats, too. Not as many as Maxi. But I sure took on problems. Then I'd get so overwhelmed, I would throw up. I'm really curious what life will be like for me now. Welcome to the world of not throwing up!"

Maybe your unskilled empath trance states haven't been so extreme. Even if you suffered just a smidge before, you need not suffer even that much. Now you have so many ways to wake up from an unskilled empath's trance and take charge of your life. Let's add one more technique to your skill set.

Break the Spell

Use our Break the Spell technique any time you're awake, unless driving a car or operating other potentially dangerous machinery.

Whenever you start to feel that you are turning your Space Dial upwards because of someone else in the room, tear your eyes away. Look at yourself. It could be a wrist, an ankle, a piece of clothing, the color of the skin on your hand, etc.

Of course, you won't look at *yourself* like a piece of furniture, right? Be interested in that chosen fragment of self. Looking at yourself, even your clothes, begin the connection. Intensify it by asking questions like these:

- How do I feel?
- Am I moving or still?
- What emotions come up when I pay attention to myself?
- What is happening in my physical body?

Anything you notice about yourself will do quite nicely to Break the Spell. Just being in the room with someone else does not mean you need slip into a hypnotic trance where that other person becomes your main reality. You never need to identify with another person unless you choose to, nor need you twirl your Space Dial all the way up to 10. Your life *is* all about you. At least it can be.

Break the Spell whenever you wish. Afterwards, when you're good and ready, go back to looking at other people in the room. They can handle your momentary lack of attention.

Actually, unless they're babies, they can handle your *long-term* lack of attention. Apart from youngsters in your care, other people seldom need your full attention.

Why? They give it to themselves.

YOUR ASSIGNMENT FOR DAY 22

Give full attention to yourself, courtesy of your eyes? Sure you can do that. Do it for the rest of today.

As needed, experiment with our shiny new techniques, Break the Spell and Eye Muscles.

Doing this assignment, Brave Explorer, you complete Part Two of your training at Empath Empowerment.

A Skilled Empath Among Friends

PART THREE:
The Fun of
Being a Skilled Empath

As a skilled empath, you become an *equal* member of the crowd. Using your skills to help others, you remain free of their pain. And you can be yourself fully. Easily. Always.

By now, you have explored many ways to be yourself, regardless of who's in the room along with you. Keeping your empath gift(s) OFF isn't done by stiffening your boundaries or any other quick gimmick. Instead, you've developed a skill set for using your consciousness. Don't you find it quite easy now, holding a space for yourself as The Most Important Person in The Room?

In ways that you wouldn't have been able to understand back at Day 1, you have so many choices. They include mind-body-spirit-intellect-soul-emotions-environment and how you direct consciousness through your eyes. No more unskilled Empath Merges for you!

So what's left to learn? In Part Three of our 30-Day Plan, you'll add exciting new skills and have more fun. Gain the full benefit of my experience, coaching thousands of empaths like you. I don't merely want you to suffer *less*. I want you to enjoy *more*.

As you refine your skills at Empath Empowerment, each day can bring new discoveries. Soon you will explore techniques to safely turn your empath gift(s) ON all the way, Space Dial set at 10.

It will be my delight, teaching you how to do a Skilled Empath Merge. Frankly, it's the biggest fun you can have with your clothes on.

Day 23. Body Language Turned Inside Out

Let's summarize your current skill set as you enter Part Three of our 30-Day Plan for Empath Empowerment. Haven't you made awesome progress at keeping your empath gift(s) turned OFF in most social situations?

Doing this will become increasingly comfortable with practice. Realistically, our plan takes 30 days, not 30 hours. But at least paying attention to yourself from the inside is growing easier, right? All the following skills can help:

1. *Paying attention to yourself* has become a more vivid and fascinating experience. In the past, maybe you were mostly alive in just one aspect of yourself, like emotions, but now you have begun to explore the full range of your very distinctive human personality: Mind-body-spirit-intellect-soul-emotions-environment.

2. Whenever you're ready for *personal growth,* you can repeat techniques from Mind Day, Body Day, etc. This will help more neglected aspects of yourself to come fully alive.

3. You know how to use spiritual consciousness to keep *evolving in a balanced way.* For continued progress, you have techniques like the Be Deep Quickie and Inner Bingo.

4. Based on familiarity with your inner resources, you have learned to *experiment with how you hold a space.* Most intensely, The Furniture Game helps your aura stay put, so you don't bounce in and out of unskilled Empath Merges. Even a few seconds of The Furniture Game can trigger an hour or more of keeping your Space Dial turned to 1.

Admittedly, keeping your Space Dial that low could still feel weird for a few more days or weeks. Soon it won't. As an empath, remember this practical equation:

My empath gift(s) turned OFF = Being The Most Important Person in The Room

Soon you won't need to cheerlead yourself to do this, muttering encouraging words to yourself, like "Furniture."

WORRIED?

Despite my reassurance, some of you Brave Explorers still may be worrying. "What if moving that Space Dial down makes me feel guilty?"

Remember, Space Dial turned to 1 is how non-empaths live most of the time. (And that doesn't make them narcissists.) Eventually, you will actually *enjoy* keeping your Space Dial at 1 most of the time. Doing so will prod you to find human-level ways to connect to others, ways that do not involve using your deepest qualities of consciousness.

Actions don't merely speak louder than words. They can take less out of you.

Here's a snapshot of everyday life for a Skilled Empath:

- When you're with others, you habitually focus on *objective* reality, seeing people and events more clearly than unskilled empaths do.
- Since you're an empath, a rich and fascinating *subjective* reality will await you whenever you make a shift inward.
- But here's the new part about your subjective reality *now.* That rich inner life doesn't require turning ON your gift(s) as an empath. You're starting to sort things out properly. An empath's gifts are meant for experiencing what it is like to be *other* people, and this is no substitute for paying attention to yourself as a regular human being.
- Interacting with people as a skilled empath, you honor yourself and advocate for yourself, acting as though your life matters. Sure, sometimes you'll become curious about other

people, like "What's with Troy and his announcement that I must watch him practice for his big audition as Macbeth?"

- But you will balance curiosity about others by giving yourself equal time. For instance, you might follow up your question about Troy with, "And what interests me now about me? What's going on in *my* mind-body-spirit-intellect-soul-emotions-environment?"

As you grow increasingly comfortable with the position of Space Dial at 1, you'll find that some of that adventurous feeling you used to get by doing unskilled Empath Merges with others... the very best of that freedom and exhilaration... can be generated at will by switching from one part of your subjective reality to another.

It's a big deal that you have all seven (Count 'em, 7!!!!!!!) inner playgrounds: Mind + body + spirit + intellect + soul + emotions + way of being in the environment.

Moving from one to another, at will, has become your standard skill set. It's like your daily bread-and-butter.

NOW ADD JELLY

As they say in the infomercials, "And there's more."

Today I want to give you a hilarious new way to turn that Space Dial to 1. Variety is sweet, like adding jelly to your bread and butter. Really, it's perfectly reasonable for us empaths to crave variety nearly as much as we crave psychic stability.

One man's deep is another man's shallow.

This ancient proverb — okay, I just made it up now — means that some things in life usually considered a big deal are actually quite puny. The difference depends on whether you're a non-empath or an empath.

Remember the wild idea, stated near the beginning of this book, that becoming a Skilled Empath can turn your reality inside out? If you're an empath, many things in life are the exact opposite of what you've been told.

Body language gives us a perfect example of the inside-out shift that's involved, going from clueless empath to Skilled Empath.

BODY LANGUAGE FOR A NON-EMPATH

Body language means studying nonverbal communication to learn more about what's going on with a person. Body language is often considered a big deal. And it is… for a non-empath. Consider our pal Troy.

- Normally, his consciousness is locked up in the four walls of his body. Other people seem like a baffling mystery.
- Even though he's used to being The Most Important Person in The Room, Troy has decided he would like to learn more about other people.
- For a non-empath like him, studying body language can help a lot. Troy can learn about people's insides from their outsides.
- To Troy, other people may never seem fully important, not compared to him. At least, body language can help him understand them a bit better.
- So Troy starts noticing items of body language, then interpreting what he sees. For him, this new knowledge will count as way deep.

But how deep is body language for you, as a born empath? Let's make a comparison. The only tricky part of this is how, in the past, you may have done extra when reading body language. Your version could really have been a more-or-less conscious Empath Merge.

Strictly speaking, body language involves paying attention to one item of facial expression or body position a time. Then you interpret what shows on the surface.

Sometimes an empath will learn about body language and use that as a springboard, much as psychics can start doing Tarot readings and transition from that into full-blown psychic readings that don't use cards at all.

So when we considering what body language means for an empath, remember that we're referring to body language alone, nothing extra.

BODY LANGUAGE FOR AN EMPATH

What can the study of body language offer an empath like you?

- Normally, your consciousness travels in and out of other people. *Locating your own self* has been the baffling mystery.
- Now you're learning to use your gift(s) on purpose, becoming The Most Important Person in The Room. Still, you long to learn more about the inner lives of people like Troy. If only there could be a way to do this and keep your Space Dial at 1.
- Ta da! It's studying body language. This kind of perception begins by focusing on someone like Troy's physical appearance. How refreshing is that? You're not noticing how he feels inside his mind-body-spirit-intellect-soul-emotions-environment but simply how he moves that obvious, outermost physical self.
- Body language helps you to gain information about Troy from a comfortable distance, while keeping your Space Dial at 1.
- To you, this new knowledge is refreshingly shallow, perfect for amusing and informing yourself while you keep your empath gift(s) turned OFF.

Think I'm kidding that body language is mostly used as something deep for non-empaths? Check out workshops and books on body language. Non-empaths can get so excited, you'd think they had found the Holy Grail.

Sales pitches for body language emphasize how the knowledge will help you to control people so you can sell them things, earn yourself money, etc. Not necessarily an empath's route to riches!

People become so excited because they can finally tell something — anything — about what happens to others on the inside.

All that glee makes sense, given what you know now about people used to being The Most Important Person in The Room.

But will funny old body language bring anyone a really deep experience of Otherness?

Otherness means the direct experience of someone or something else like a crystal or plant. Instead of emphasizing your distinctive versions of mind-body-spirit-intellect-soul-emotions-environment, instead of having your usual habits of relying on some of these categories more than others, with Otherness you move into a different way of having consciousness. Because every person, plant, animal, crystal, machine, earth environment does have its own distinctive consciousness.

To experience Otherness, a non-empath would need to study Aura Reading. Then Otherness will come in the form of information. (By contrast, for an empath who reads auras, Otherness comes as a direct, personal experience.)

Body language won't really give a non-empath knowledge of Otherness. Instead, there's information at a superficial level. At least, observing body language can move a non-empath in a deeper direction.

The Body Language Game

Now that you're oriented, here how to play with our latest technique for Empath Empowerment.

Whenever you start to notice a person's body language, remember that physical bodies are perceived at the surface of life.

So the act of noticing body positions and expression can be a way to shift your consciousness up to the surface of reality. Automatically, your Space Dial will re-set at 1.

1. Notice one specific item at a time. (Examples will follow.)
2. Set the intention to stay on the surface, reading expression and body position.
3. Figure out the meaning of your specific item. Develop your own system. Or, if you've been reading a body language book with someone else's system, consider if the suggested interpretation seems true to you. Evaluating in that way can help to fine tune your interpretations.
4. With no effort, your Space Dial will re-set at 1.

HAND BEHAVIOR

The following body language insights come from another book of mine, *Read People Deeper*, published by Women's Intuition Worldwide, Page 230.

1. Observe how your partner moves hands while talking. Are they flexible, stiff, forceful, sensitive, creative, responsive? (Yes, hands can definitely be considered phallic symbols.)
2. A partner who prizes sensuousness will show it in *grooming,* especially of hands.
3. They're vital sensual tools So it's revealing to see if they're either showcased or neglected. How much care has gone into the nails? Have those hands been kept clean?
4. Wallowing in dirt can be sensuous, too. Be honest about what appeals to you.
5. *Touch quality,* from those very same hands, is another tip-off to sensuousness. How does your partner handle objects? Watch him/her pick up car keys or hold a glass of water.
6. Do sparks fly when your partner's fingers make contact with your body? Be it a handshake, a shoulder pat, or a caress of your cheek, some hands shine like spotlights for *physical intelligence.*
7. Other kinds of sensuousness show that a person is *awake intuitively.* Does your partner's hand seem to read your emotions, your energy, your sexual interest, how you feel physically?
8. Especially if you are a Skilled Empath, you can tell another empath by touch. Are you, the relationship reader, being read?

YOUR ASSIGNMENT FOR DAY 23

Your assignment for today is to purposely play the Body Language Game. Read other people, right on the surface. Do this at least three times. Before and after, notice how you feel. Don't you remain yourself, STUFF-free?

One quick reading of body language is enough to twirl your Space Dial back to 1. If you were born as an empath, that is what body language does best.

Day 24. First-Date
Somebody Wonderful

Married? Single? Leading a double life, or a triple one? Regardless, today's assignment can suit you just fine. Keep your lifestyle. Just start dating somebody new.

For the adventurous, dating always opens up interesting possibilities . Haven't you heard amazing stories about first dates? Here's one that I heard:

MELVIN AS SOUL MATE

"Melvin and I met for drinks after work. Then we went back to my place to talk. We talked. We made love. We talked more, until 3:00 in the morning.

"After we woke up, we started talking again. It was so wonderful, we could hardly tear ourselves away to go to work. That's how it has been between us ever since. Melvin is my soul mate."

Well, here's a contrasting tale about dating. Susie and John are entering a party. They've been together a very long time and are making their game plan for this event.

PLANNING FOR A MOST UNROMANTIC DATE

John: "Why should I bother with talking to you at this party? Much as I love you, let's admit it. We already know everything about each other.

"The whole point of a party is the new blood. I'm going to join the conversation over there, and don't you dare follow me. Find your own people."

Susie: "I couldn't agree more. Leave me alone while I explore what makes these people tick. I've got to. Staying with you, I could die of boredom."

Guess what? A version of Susie and John's conversation probably occurs regularly within your own subconscious mind. Empaths can treat *themselves* like a long-suffering spouse, so very taken for granted.

HOW DO YOU TALK TO YOURSELF, PAL?

Look, you have been making great progress at turning your empath gift(s) OFF. You're having thrilling conversations. You have carried out *Melvin as Cupid*-like encounters with your own mind-body-spirit-intellect-soul-emotions-environment.

Altogether, you're more than halfway there, falling in love with yourself as The Most Important Person in The Room.

But sometimes doesn't it still feel empty, paying so much attention to yourself? As if life without constant empathic travel into other people's auras could make you boring!

Well, you're never really boring, not for a minute. But how you treat yourself as a person... that could definitely be boring.

Consider this possibility. You might be due to upgrade you self-dating. How do you treat yourself in your spare time?

Whenever you find yourself even slightly bored with yourself today, you can actively start to first-date yourself. Here's what I mean.

Start to First-Date Yourself

Act interested in yourself. Don't wait for Mr. Right or Ms. Right to suddenly materialize to do the job for you. No more searching for Melvin! Instead, ask yourself questions, the kind you would ask on a good first date. Answer every question enthusiastically and keep the ball rolling:

* Looking around where we are right now, what looks really good to you?
* You're right, that *is* beautiful.
* Do you like sports? What do you think of those Mets?
* Interesting! Your perspective is so refreshing. Now, I've heard you also have quite the brain for politics. What do you think is the most important issue in our country today?

> Yes, this is to be a non-stop conversation, as with sombody new who is absolutely fascinating.
>
> Assume that you want to know all about this promising new date. Ask plenty of questions. And don't be shy about revealing yourself. Answer those questions. Put all your feelings into words. Scatter opinions liberally, just like your praise:
>
> - Clever!
> - Outrageous!
> - Aw, you're so witty. What makes you think that?

Silly, yes. I'll admit it. First-dating yourself can seem outrageously silly. You might even talk aloud to yourself more than normal.

However, if you're even moderately observant, you'll notice that plenty of other people talk to themselves, too. And they're not having nearly as good a time.

Why? They're just mumbling to self like a burned-out old spouse. You, by contrast, are on a fabulous first date.

WHY YOU WIN

We're talking about a *successful* first date, naturally. Dating yourself today, the intent isn't to practice your sneer.

A winning first date includes sincere curiosity. You're curious and respectful, more apt to praise than to blame.

Frankly, unskilled-empaths can act more like promiscuous, frantic daters of any random stranger in the room. Say that James is at a Seven Eleven. It's located far away from home. Waiting in line, he notices Wilhelmina, someone he'll never see again, let alone date. Yet standing in line to buy his Diet Coke, in his consciousness, James could be first-dating like crazy:

- Hey, Wilhelmina, what's it like to be you?
- How do you feel emotionally, Wilhelmina, my new buddy?
- Can I send you some energy?
- Long as I'm popping in and out of your aura, why don't I take on some of your pain?

- No need to thank me.
- Waiting in line, I'll casually monitor your thinking process. Nice job.

Or sometimes an unskilled empath like James will stand in line and lament that he *doesn't* have a date with Wilhelmina (or anyone else).

- Here I am stuck in line at this pathetic Seven Eleven. Alone again. If only I were on a date, it wouldn't be so bad. We'd have fun. Even here, we'd manage to have fun somehow.
- Will I always be alone?
- Where, oh where, is my soul mate?

Never again need you be bored with your companion — especially when that companion is you. Never again need you treat yourself like an estranged spouse, so full of resentment that you could go out to dinner with S.O. and be so bored, you eat in hostile silence.

If they choose, any couple can treat each other with first-date curiosity. Well, you can treat yourself that way, too.

Admittedly there are other cures for boredom. If you can't stand being alone with yourself, you might benefit from some professional help from the healer of your choice.

Or you could simply cover your naked body with sliced salami (for the variety). But my recommendation for today is the following technique. It's simple, cheap and relatively inconspicuous.

First-Dating on Your Big Night

Imagine, if it were Prom Night, or some other ultra-festive occasion, wouldn't you be on your best behavior?
Bring that attitude when you first-date yourself. Notice that person's adorable body, sparkling intellect, loving heart.
Compliments would be appreciated.
Get to know this marvellous person further by asking loads of questions.

> - What do you think of this place?
> - Sure I'm interested. I *want* to know your opinion. Why do you have that reaction?
> - Absolutely right! What else do you think?
>
> Answer each question enthusiastically, even if it's just a running commentary about routine errands.

And you know what's especially freeing about this kind of date? You can say all you want about ME-ME-ME and never risk seeming too interested in yourself!

First-date yourself a few times each day, seeing your life through fresh eyes. You'll build self-esteem and gratitude, appreciate what you've got going for you.

Whatever happened in your childhood, however much attention parents did or didn't give you, and regardless of the present state of your love life, you can make this a great first date!

Have more of them tomorrow and happily ever after.

YOUR ASSIGNMENT FOR DAY 24

Show interest in yourself as a person and first-date yourself. Do it at least twice today, each time for two minutes or longer.

If you want to be extra fancy, try the Be Deep Quickie both before and after.

Before you try this assignment, Brave Explorer, paying so much attention to yourself, out loud, may seem silly. But first-dating yourself may prove surprisingly helpful.

What if the relationship develops into a real love match? You just might wind up joyfully, powerfully aware of YOU, Space Dial set at 1.

Day 25. Grounding or Jail

Being an Empowered Empath is not a weird lifestyle. Zachary 's bathroom, with his surprising array of grooming products, now, that's a weird lifestyle. Empaths stay clear by subtle shifts of consciousness, not by using their own distinctive blend of hair spray and Miracle Gro.

As a Skilled Empath, you're invited to make subtle changes to your lifestyle. Even tiny changes, like the occasional First-Date Yourself, can make it easier to keep your empath gift(s) OFF most of the time.

Starting Day 28, this new lifestyle will become a basis for turning your empath gift(s) ON. It's your birthright to do Skilled Empath Merges as desired, and do them safely without taking on other people's STUFF. Soon, but not yet!

Meanwhile, *grounding* is today's term to sum up the Turn OFF part of that lifestyle. Grounding means fully inhabiting your body and the rest of your human life… as if it were real and you liked it.

Sex is not the only way this can happen. For almost every activity in life, you can choose a version that is grounding.

By contrast, turning empath gift(s) ON means *expanding spiritually.* Many other choices and habits cause expansion, like playing music, texting friends, eating sweets, drinking wine. They're pleasurable because expansion brings a high.

Nevertheless, expansion comes at a price. One way or another, you will need to integrate every bit of that expansion. If you don't do this voluntarily, life will do it to you. This won't be pretty.

Remember before you started our 30-Day Plan? If you're like most of my students, you had the habit of expanding so often with unskilled Empath Merges, you couldn't comfortably keep up with the integrating part.

Whooshing in and out of others with your aura may feel like "me," but it's really a matter of lifestyle, a habit. Alas, the habit of "not being in your surroundings or body" can come back to bite you.

DRAMA VS. GENTLER INVITATIONS

Huge weight gain, inability to stop smoking, chronic pain, poverty, Zachary's reluctance to shampoo — problems like these can be pretty dramatic warnings about being ungrounded.

Think of stories you've heard where drama was blamed on bad luck: So-called "accidents," getting fired for "no reason," health problems that come "out of nowhere." In seemingly random ways, someone you care about becomes a victim. Only maybe he or she isn't a victim so much as a person who didn't listen to life's gentler invitations.

Think about Zachary, going through a stage where he isn't grounded enough to function effectively in everyday life. Since he doesn't much value objective reality, how will he notice life's subtler hints that he's off balance? How can life let Zachary know when there is a problem?

That's one reason (not the only reason, but a surprisingly common one) why bad things happen to good people. Drama can be God's way of remaining anonymous.

Suppose that Zachary isn't in his body much, consciously. That body can't tap him on the shoulder and holler "Hellooooo" to grab his attention. Instead, he'll attract very attention-grabbing events from outside himself (a.k.a. Drama).

Brave Explorer, accept life's kinder invitations. Develop the habit of paying attention to your body and environment, especially when unusual things happen around you. When your lifestyle balances expansion with plenty of grounding, you'll attract less drama.

Once you decide to pay attention to life's gentle invitations, you may notice more of them happening. Good!

For instance, say that you lock yourself out of the house. Again. Don't just stomp your feet angrily once you have managed to get inside the front door. Consider yourself warned: More grounding may be needed.

Here's a personal example of an invitation to become more grounded. Once I managed to drop my watch down the kitchen sink.

Not only did this ruin my device for measuring human time. Since I was too spaced out to notice when or where the watch slid off my wrist, later I had to bring in a repairman to fix the garbage disposal.

Turns out, garbage disposals don't like to chew up wristwatches. Throwing human timekeeping device in the garbage? Nice symbolic touch! It was a pretty strong invitation to ground myself more.

What difference does it make to notice your invitations? If you suspect that more grounding is needed, do something extra for grounding. You can become a person who sprinkles plenty of delicious bits of grounding into each day. Here's a list of choices.

THE BIG LIST FOR GROUNDING

The Spaced Out Choice	The Grounding Choice
Meditate only on your chakras, the energy of the universe, or transcending your body altogether.	Include time in your meditation to feel your physical body or to explore your connection to Mother Earth.
Arrive at appointments whenever you're in the mood.	Be — or become — punctual.
Spend money whenever you feel like it.	Stick to a budget.
Waking up, go through your morning routine on autopilot, e.g., You barely notice your body until you have filled up at the coffee pump.	Use every part of your morning routine to re-establish your mind-body connection, e.g., When you brush your teeth, notice that you have teeth.
Check messages on your cell and your email more often than noticing that you have feet.	For every time that you turn on technology (computer, phone, a new I-Tune), give yourself 30 seconds to wiggle your toes.

Breath is something to notice only if you're out of it.	At least once per hour, take a loooong, sloooow, mindful deep breath.
So far, you have never learned how to relax your body on purpose.	Figure out ways to intentionally relax your body, such as stretching, blinking extra and then returning to normal, breathing extra-deeply and then returning to normal, adjusting your posture. Occasionally ask your body "What would feel good to you right now?" Then do it.
When food tempts you, it must be eaten. It's as though food can become The Most Important Person in The Room. (Actually, just because food is around does not make it more powerful than your own body's needs. No food has the power to force you to eat it.)	You notice when you are hungry versus when you are full. With food, as with people, you make yourself The Most Important Person in The Room. When deciding whether or not to eat, you consult your whole body, not just your taste buds.
Your diet lavishly emphasizes uppers like sugar, white flour, and alcohol. But you're stingy with downers, like protein, complex carbs, and oils.	Your diet emphasizes grounders like protein, complex carbs, and oils. Your diet is stingy with trippy foods like sugar, simple carbs, alcohol.
When choosing health aids, like vitamins and aromatherapy oils, you select products based on someone else's "supposed to," a theory. Or else you have some authority figure choose for you.	When choosing health aids, like vitamins and aromatherapy oils, you select products based on what feels good to your own personal body.

You pay attention to your body only if it hurts.	Voluntarily notice your body at random times all day long, just for fun. (You'll never have a better friend than your physical body.)
Before going to sleep at night, you can't wait to pray or worry over your two favorite problems. Or, perhaps, you count sheep and your sexual conquests.	Before going to sleep at night, you notice your body. You pay attention. "Dearest body, how you doing? How do you feel?" That body has supported a whole day's worth of activity. Would it be so terrible to send it a "Thank you?"

WHY GROUNDING IS NOT CENTERING

Many of my students have heard that the solution to many of life's problems is "to find your center" or "to move into your center." You too? Then admit it. Don't you have trouble remembering to do this?

Bosh! Don't blame your memory. Blame the very concept of "centering."

What's wrong with it? You don't possess only one center. You have many, remember?

So what happens when a person tries to center? If you find this easy and helpful, more power to you. But usually trying to center means moving consciousness to the one category where you feel most comfortable.

Sure, this strategy is preferable to paying attention to all the other people in the room. Still, if you're out of balance within yourself, centering within that one category will only worsen the imbalance.

Centering is like saying, "I have a store where I can go to recharge and buy breath mints. It's called Emotion World." (Substitute whichever category of yourself *used* to be your main specialty before you started using this 30-Day Plan.)

Actually, you're not just one store. You're a franchise. You own:

- Mind World
- Body World
- Spirit World
- Intellect World
- Soul World
- Emotion World and
- Environment World

So don't limit your sense of who-am-I to one of those stores. And definitely don't confuse any form of centering with fully grounding yourself. The latter requires visiting Body World, Mind World, Soul World and Environment World.

Most unskilled empaths, having the habit of being over-subjective, prefer Emotion World, Intellect World and/or Spirit World.

So don't just center yourself. Ground yourself. Do this even though the idea of getting up close and personal with Body World plus Environment World can bring up a raging fear of jail.

GET OUT OF JAIL FREE

Ever play Monopoly? Then you know the thrill of a *Get Out of Jail Free* card.

Real life involves playing a game, too (hopefully, not a bored game). Alas, many empaths forget that we ever agreed to play the game of living on earth. Instead we feel as though we've been thrown in jail.

Why? Life on earth is gross. Timing is slow. We must poop — and I'm not referring here to The Big Analogy. Some of us earthling empaths are so grossed out by life that guess what happens?

We resist being in our bodies with all our might. Yet bodies aren't just something to keep around grudgingly, like a pesky kid brother.

We resist the environment by being over-subjective. (Ironically, this makes us ineffective at objective things like earning a living or scoring a date. Such a vicious cycle!)

Ambivalent living shows in auras. Born empaths live primarily from the Heart Chakra up. Until we establish a strong presence in the lower chakras, to so-called "normal" people we can seem diminished energetically.

Why would "normal" people notice an aura imbalance in us? Consider Exhibit A, Roscoe.

- Like most non-empaths, patterns in his aura show that he comes alive mostly at the Root Chakra.
- Back during puberty, a second large display developed in Roscoe's Belly Chakra.
- Now that he's an adult, this Belly Chakra expands any time he gets a crush; otherwise it's puny.
- Finally, Roscoe might possibly develop a bit of action at the Solar Plexus Chakra, especially when he's acting like a power freak.

At best, that means Roscoe has three big, lively chakras out of the main seven chakras. Does his pattern have anything in common with your own aura right now?

Not much, until you are *fully* skilled as an empath. All the Empath Empowerment skills you've learned before today, important as they are, don't necessarily change chakra proportions. Until your lifestyle includes lots of grounding, your aura may be big exactly in those chakras where Roscoe and most other people are small — at the Heart Chakra, Third Eye Chakra, Crown Chakra.

Say that unskilled empath Meg and non-empath Roscoe go out for dinner. Will she be the respected buddy who gets to eat her fair share of the pizza? Not with that aura contrast. Are you kidding?

Neither the Megs nor the Roscoes of the world are likely to *consciously* notice this chakra mismatch problem (or how her side of the mismatch relates to resisting life).

Conscious aura reading is optional, great but optional. Regardless, everyone has a Higher Self that *does* read auras. At that level, Meg will respond to Roscoe's aura and he will respond to hers. (The term I've developed for this is *auric modeling*.)

Because of auric modeling, when Meg's aura has such different proportions, the Roscoes of the world will treat her like a second-class citizen. She might (wrongly) be considered "inauthentic."

But with grounding, Meg's — or your — chakra proportions will change. You'll add a big presence at the lower chakras. Meanwhile, you'll keep the big higher chakras. Every empath can develop a full set of healthy, balanced chakras. That, in turn, can bring you a fabulous life in the classroom.

EMBRACE LIFE AT EARTH SCHOOL

Grounding more could really change your life. Yet I just know some of you Brave Explorers aren't quite convinced yet of the need for full grounding. Here's a deeper perspective that could help.

This place I call "Earth School" is easy to love but easier to hate. The place is soooooooooo darned slow.

Actually, it is slow for a reason. At our quaint little academy, various illusions and tempos enhance the learning.

- Our bodies appear to be *who* we are, although really we are energy beings having a human experience.
- Our bodies appear to be *separate* from the bodies of other people, plants, animals, etc. – ridiculous since, as you very well know, unskilled empaths fly in and out of other people's subtle bodies constantly. (For more information about how separate bodies are an illusion, ask your friendly neighborhood quantum physicist.)
- *Fear and pain* seemingly threaten to "kill" our bodies. Actually, your soul is indestructible. You will always be living in some body, somewhere. (Ask your friendly neighborhood regression therapist.)

Here is what I have found, doing healing sessions with empaths from many parts of the world. You may fear grounding most because, seemingly, it would isolate you more than ever from God.

Fighting the illusions of earth, a born empath does frequent quick Empath Merges, moving in and out of other people's auras. This feels comforting, even if afterwards you bring back other people's STUFF into your aura.

But here's the bigger truth about living on earth. You're already connected to God and the rest of humanity. Full willingness to be

human — without holding back — will help you to enjoy that connection more.

Already you may have noticed that living with your gift(s) turned
OFF helps you to become more comfy in your body and environment. Gone are the days when you connected to others only as God's
humble (and, possibly, frantic) servant. Then you would merge away
constantly, picking up random STUFF. Now you get to calmly establish a real-life identity as a human being.

Here at Earth School, every thought, word and action produces
consequences. They out-picture in what happens to us, our health,
relationships, the amount of roadkill encountered while driving down
life's highway. In order for Earth to be effective as a school, we must be
willing to accept these out-pictured consequences as if they were real,
even important.

Given how life here works, choosing to be born as an empath
was heroically brave. Look at the faces and bodies, even the auras, of
most people who evolve at Earth School over the decades.

- By age five, the glow is usually gone.
- By mid-life, most of us look like we have been twirled
  around in a food processor.
- By 65 and beyond, many of us develop faces that look like
  beat-up hiking boots.

We beings who incarnate at Earth School are the marines of the universe. More power to us, even if most of us don't credit our full learning until the big Life Review at the end!

Unskilled empaths suffer *more* than most, even as Skilled
Empaths suffer *less* than most. Why? Think consequences.

What consequences flow when we empaths don't fully accept
being here? They ain't pretty.

So don't fear caring too much about your body or other aspects
of human life. Will it cut you off from God? Will you risk losing
oneness with people, plants and animals? Brave Explorer, I'm here to
tell you, this can't possibly happen.

+ Big perspective: Earth School's illusions won't last. At the end of this life you'll be outta here, feeling much lighter, as if all that dieting had finally worked. Even before you entered this lifetime, you were a big, evolved consciousness. Otherwise you couldn't have come in as an empath, period. Life at Earth School as an empath is designed to add to your spiritual stature, not diminish it.

• Immediate perspective: It is totally safe to jump in. Starting today, you can fully inhabit your body, your surroundings, your human connections with people. Doing this, you'll evolve faster, not slower. Ironically your spiritual connection will grow far stronger.

YOUR ASSIGNMENT FOR DAY 25

Consider, are you going to play here on earth as a good sport from now on?

What's your alternative? I would never recommend suicide… but you might wish to seek seclusion by locking yourself in Zachary's bathroom for the next 10 years or so.

Otherwise, be a good sport. Be here now. Be here fully, which requires grounding.

Your assignment for today is to do at least three things from our Big List for Grounding. Or else find other ways to get grounded. These can be variations on what you already do.

Just be sure to include at least half an hour of physical exercise daily, because your body will accept no substitute.

Day 26. Greed

Greed and vanity no longer are fashionable sins, which is a pity. Ask Meg. Once upon a past lifetime, she worked for the Catholic church. She sold "indulgences." Depending on how well people controlled the seven deadly sins, indulgences became excellent income streams for Meg. That's one reason to like greed.

Of course, post-modern culture gives us plenty of other reasons. Advertisers are paid to persuade us that although greed is good, more greed is better.

Actually, the very moment in life when you're thinking, "I like this and want a lot more" may be the precise moment when your inner self has been trying to signal you that "I've had plenty already. More would be a mistake."

Only most of us never have learned to read those signals. Really, when was the last time that you saw a TV commercial for... satisfaction.

Outsmart Greed

For a Skilled Empath, the moment when you feel "I want more" or "I want faster" is precisely the time to pause. Take. A. Breath. Ask inside, "What's happening inside me right now?"
If you do this, very often you'll hear/see/feel, "I've had enough. What I have now is plenty. All I need do is stop and enjoy what I have."

That's the antidote to greed, *awareness of enough*. Sometimes this is called "gratitude," other times "smart." But what if your best word for it is "hard"?

GETTING PAST GREED

Why should greed matter so much to an empath? You're close, so very close, to mastering the fine art of turning your empath gift(s) OFF as a matter of habit. Through your grounded lifestyle, your chakras are becoming more balanced. Grounding canimprove relationships and your financial prospects, too. So you're doing great!

Soon — day after tomorrow, actually — I'll show you how to jet-propel your consciousness into another person, full force, a.k.a. turning your gift(s) ON.

How fascinating will that be, doing Skilled Empath Merge at will? I consider it the biggest fun you can have with your clothes on. But even then, will you feel as though you have traveled enough?

Sure, unless you give way to that last little smidge of subconscious greed. It's the shadow side of enthusiasm.

Teaching workshops, I've found that greed can arise in ways that don't make much sense consciously. Here are some examples:

Greed shows up when, midway through the morning, Zachary is multi-tasking. He thinks he's being oh-so-cool, checking messages while he listens to the class with just one ear.

What he doesn't know: Using only part of your mind, you can't succeed at empath TURN OFF techniques. Or TURN ON techniques. You know why, don't you? Which (intellect) part of his mind-body-spirit-intellect-soul-emotions-environment self is Zachary using when he multi-tasks, anyway?

Jocelyn wants to be the class superstar. So she's reading ahead, skimming, impatient to bypass the boring parts and get to the good stuff.

What she doesn't know: A skill is not just an idea but something to experience. Preparation and refinement can be necessary for introducing a genuinely new experience.

That's certainly true about becoming a Skilled Empath. If you want to complete your training fully, settle into the here and now. Follow the sequence of instruction. It has been designed as it is for a reason.

Greed means wanting to have more than you have. More than the others in the class. Or faster than other people plodding through a 30-Day Plan.

Seven Lively Greed Reducers

Here are seven simple ways to break the habit of greed. If you like, think of this technique collection as an antidote to the Seven Deadly Sins.

Each Reducer can help you to feel more serene, enjoying your life just the way it is. As a side effect, you'll automatically keep your empath gift(s) OFF.

Read through as much of the list as you like. Then choose one — only one — technique to do at a time. Pushing yourself to do all seven simultaneously might be greedy. It certainly would be impossible.

1. Spend one minute thinking about things you are grateful for. (If you do this aloud, you'll intensify the gratitude.)

2. Jump-start full awareness of your *physical body* — in case it has been left behind in your quest for rapture. Give yourself a well-placed, gentle pinch.

Once that pinch ends, let yourself notice: "Here and now, my body is a source of bliss."

3. Jump-start full awareness of your *mind* — in case it has been marginalized yet again in pursuit of "There's gotta be more."

Ask yourself, "What do I choose to remember about this moment?"

Note: If you're worried about losing your memory with age, be especially enthusiastic about spending time at the level of your mind, not voraciously straining to find anything extra but simply enjoying the here and now.

4. Jump-start full use of your *intellect* — in case it has been bored. Plain vanilla here-and-now can be full of fascination. To stir up the fun, ask one question at a time.

5. Jump-start full awareness of your *emotions* — in case they are stuck on something un-pleasurable which causes you to want more, more, more of something different. (Might some residual greed have you demanding that every moment be the

emotional equivalent of eating candy?) Gently acknowledge your current emotion, whatever it is, by asking yourself, "What do I feel right now?"

Then notice it. Don't try to change it. Simple, loving acknowledgment with your conscious mind can cause deeper healing in the long run.

6. Jump-start your *soul* — in case it has been dozing. Make a wish. The nature of your soul is perfection, delight, freedom, plenty. Wishes allow your soul to speak to the rest of you.

7. And, of course, you can always use this powerful new *whole-self* technique:

Take a deep breath. Then ask yourself, "What is happening inside me right now?"

Whatever you find, it's highly unlikely that it will be the greed slogan, "I need more."

YOUR ASSIGNMENT FOR DAY 26

As your Empath Coach, asking you to clean up every last bit of subconscious greed might be asking too much. Might even be considered greedy on my part!

So let's make today's assignment simple. Just for one day, 24 hours, *be open to releasing any habitual greed that blocks your becoming a fully skilled empath.*

Whatever you're doing today, either do it or not, nothing in between. And decide when you've done it enough.

Grounding choices, as discussed yesterday, are important. But apart from making those wise choices, you can only *stay* grounded if you develop the habit of turning your empath gift(s) OFF and enjoying yourself in the moment. Without greed.

Day 27. Room of Requirement

As of today, you officially own the necessary skills of an empath: You know what your empath gift(s) are. Plus you know how to keep them turned OFF. In this new lifestyle, everyone in the room is important, yourself included. And, with a slight shift of awareness, you can transform yourself into The Most Important Person in the Room.

Now let's see how relaxed you can be about this new way of life. Greed is going, going, gone. But do you have old habits of self-protectiveness or hiding that are no longer needed? To be perfectly safe and secure as an empath, all you really need is to be yourself, using the power of your consciousness.

Choose to be grounded. Let that consciousness fill up that full Bingo card. That, plus all the other skills you've been mastering, will help you to be yourself a way that comes across to others as natural and powerful.

But what if you're still worried? What if you want one more something to help shield yourself from taking on STUFF? As a skilled empath, some days you know you'll be dealing with difficult people, like Roscoe's girlfriend Tiger. Isn't there any extra precaution you can take? Here comes our final empath's Turn OFF technique.

HOGWARTS SELF-STUDY

Thank you, J.K. Rowling for all the education I've received from Hogwarts. I know you didn't write all those Harry Potter books as do-it-yourself manuals. But thanks to you, I have learned a lot about banishing boggarts and conjuring up a patronus. Mostly I'm in love with your concept of a "Room of Requirement."

Even a squib (someone woefully untalented at magic) can conjure one up easily. All you need is a need. Once you make your request, this special room will take form exactly the way you require it to be.

Create a Room of Requirement

Ideally, you'll create this Room of Requirement *before* you have contact with a difficult person like Tiger, the mud wrestler. Otherwise, excuse yourself for a moment and use a restroom stall as an emergency fix-up place. With practice, you can create an empath's Room of Requirement in less than one minute.

1. Prepare to go within. Sit comfortably and close your eyes.
2. Notice how it feels to be you right now. Anything you notice is fine. Whatever you're noticing is about *you*, and that's the point.
3. Imagine, visualize or simply think about standing outside a Room of Requirement. This could be a complete building or a cozy apartment.
It could be simple or fancy. It could be shaped like your body, a pyramid, igloo, etc. Make the walls any color and material you like.
And let's emphasize that word *like*. Since the décor comes absolutely free of charge, indulge yourself.
4. Be sure to add a front door through which you can enter. Then go inside.
5. As you stand inside this Room of Requirement, again notice how it feels to be you.
6. Bring in the Divine Being of your choice. As always, worship or special rituals are optional.
7. After offering any greeting you like — including none at all — ask, "Will you please help me today?"
8. You're sure to receive an okay. Divine Beings give unconditional love and support whenever we ask. But don't wait to receive some big, official "***Y***E***S***", like a cartoon sledgehammer that knocks Tweety Bird to the ground.

Any technique or prayer that you do involving a Divine Being needs no big drama in order to count as real.

9. Continuing, say, "Please protect me all day and night. If any STUFF starts to come into me from other people, take it. Help that person if he or she wishes to accept that help. I definitely accept your help. Always keep me clear."

10. Long as you're making requests, you might wish to add a help list, such as, "Also, please send healing energy to everyone in my family and my 17 cats."

Add anything else to the conversation you wish. (But you already figured that out on your own, right?)

11. Something special will happen soon. Count aloud from one to three. Then your Room of Requirement will quickly shrink in size, shrinking more with each number, until it merges with your skin.

Okay, say those numbers now: 1, 2, 3.

12. Now you're surrounded by this miniaturized Room of Requirement. How far does it stick out? No thicker than a dewdrop. And that's all you need do in order to receive this form of protection. Open your eyes.

Most days, you won't feel the need to create a Room of Requirement. But it's nice to have the skill when you want it. Another plus is that maid service for this protective room can be yours for free. Just use the following optional technique.

Clean Your Room of Requirement

Before you go to sleep, take a moment to release and recharge your Room of Requirement.

1. Close your eyes in preparation for going within.

2. Imagine, visualize or simply think about your dewdrop-fine Room of Requirement. To release it you will count aloud from three to one. Your Room will then *expand* in size, more with each number, springing back to its original dimensions.

3. Okay, say those numbers now: 3, 2, 1.

4. Imagine walking out through the door.

5. Think the name of the Divine Being who helped you create the Room of Requirement. Ask Him or Her to clean it up after you're gone.

Alternatively, you could design the Room as self-cleaning. If only human engineers had that same power of command!

6. Spend a few seconds thinking about, visualizing or imagining how that cleanup could work. Choose a sprinkler system, a magical waterfall, fairy dust with suction powers... whatever you like.

7. Thank the Divine Being. (It's only polite.)

8. Pay attention to your body and environment. Open your eyes.

What happens if you forget to clean your Room of Requirement?

That won't be a problem. Remember who's inside there? A Divine Being like St. Francis does good work. And, over time, he will only smell better. After a few days, he'll cause your Room of Requirement to dematerialize, along with any STUFF in it.

Cleaning that Room is mostly a way to empower yourself as a co-creator with God. Plus it's fun.

Congratulations on learning how to create, release and clean up your own Room of Requirement. Now you have that extra bit of personal protection, as needed.

YOUR ASSIGNMENT FOR DAY 27

Adding our Room of Requirement techniques is an optional change to your routine. Just for today, practice the pair of techniques. Create the room now. Before you go to sleep, clean it. With this bit of practice, you will own this skill set for life.

The biggest protection, however, is simpler than creating a Room of Requirement. For an empath, the biggest protection is just being yourself, empath gift(s) turned OFF — you in all your glory.

Day 28. Magic Picture

Your first official Skilled Empath Merge — yes, you'll do it today.

You're ready now. Not only will you stay in better balance than if you'd tried today's technique earlier. The quality of your experience will be better. And the information you receive will be more accurate.

It's like the reason why psychiatrists must go through therapy before becoming qualified to practice. *Helping other people, you can only go as deep as you have gone into yourself.*

Deep/shallow: You've been playing around with these concepts while exploring what it means to become The Most Important Person in The Room. You have learned to relish, in depth, each category of your mind-body-spirit-intellect-soul-emotions-environment.

Today's turn ON technique for your empath gift(s) can take you *that* deeply and widely into the person with whom you do the Empath Merge.

So roll up your sleeves. Loosen your belt. Make whatever adjustments to clothing signify your readiness to start something special. Zachary, for instance, needs to snap his suspenders so they make a rich twanging sound.

Learning your first technique for Skilled Empath Merge, you will need a full 30 minutes — uninterrupted. Unless you have that time right now, stop reading. Return when you do have that time. Most of it will be needed for preparation. Doing the technique itself will take you 10 minutes or less.

PREPARE FOR MAGIC

The official name of this technique is Magic Picture. Nothing about today's technique is difficult. But results will be yours only on this condition: Go with me step by step. Like it or not, there is no way to do Safe, Deep and Skilled Empath Merge for Dummies.

MAGIC SUPPLIES

For starters, Magic Picture will demand certain supplies:

1. The previously-mentioned 30 minutes of your precious time
2. A room where you will be uninterrupted by cell phone, pets, a panting roommate who just can't wait to have sex with you, etc.
3. A recording device, whether that be an electronic machine to record your voice or good old-fashioned pen and paper
4. A certain kind of photograph (to be described soon)

Photos are great for doing Skilled Empath Merges. Photos don't talk back or giggle. They won't rush you or make you self-conscious in any way. This holds true whether you choose a photo of somebody you know well or a total stranger.

FIND AN EXCELLENT PHOTO

Here are the specs for the best kind of photo to select for the Magic Picture technique.

1. Have only one person in your photo.
2. That would be a human person, not a poodle or extra terrestrial, not a cartoon of Daffy Duck.
3. Your person must be facing the camera at a nice clear front angle. This image should go all the way down to the waist. Longer is fine, shorter is not.
4. Nothing about the person's physical appearance should be distracting. So probably the person in your photo will be wearing clothing. Now, Zachary has a real fondness for the swimsuit issue of Sports Illustrated; he is soooo into those cute bathing suits. But enjoying photos like these would be considered a different technique.

5. For pity's sake, choose a photo of somebody nice, not too appetizing but also not revolting. Avoid that politician you love to hate from the front page of today's newspaper.
6. Not to be too demanding, but your photo should also be larger than a postage stamp.
7. You'll be learning about the person *at the time of the photograph.* If you want to merge with Troy as an adult, don't use that cute baby picture. Find something current.

Whew, now we have all that settled, let's practice the physical positioning for this technique.

POSITION MATTERS

Any conscious, intentional Empath Merge counts as a big deal. Treat the process with respect and you'll receive the most accurate information possible. You'll be of service to the greatest extent possible. And you'll be fully protected against STUFF going into your aura.

Begin by paying attention to your physical position. Do what you can to ensure you will not be interrupted by a phone, a person, or anything else. Take away cigarettes or gum. Keep your undivided attention.

Now, sit comfortably in a chair, feet on the floor, legs not crossed, arms not crossed.

Hold your photo in one hand and lift it up until you can see the person in your picture at eye level.

Is your photo on a computer screen? Any laptop belongs off your lap. Adjust positions relative to where you sit to get the screen image eye level. Do whatever scrolling, etc., is needed so you can sit across from that image comfortably, head erect and eyes looking straight ahead.

Most of us are used to looking down at pictures. That won't work well for any Empath Merge technique. Your brain processes information differently when you look on the level versus looking down.

Can you look over now, at eye level, and see your person's forehead? How about the neck? Even a short neck will do.

Excellent! Photo practice is over, so put your photo down, or turn away from your screen, and keep reading.

ABOUT THAT RECORDING DEVICE

We've already noted that you will be record your experiences with Magic Picture. Probably you'll just scribble quick notes on a sheet of paper, although you could make a sound recording.

To give yourself the best possible experience, tell yourself right now that this process is going to be quick and easy. Ideally, making notes during a technique like this is just like drooling. No need to pretty anything up, more like a spontaneous, automatic response. Decide right now that when you do this technique you will:

- Never stop to check that your writing is pretty.
- Forget about making grammatically correct sentences.
- Just make enough of a scribble to be readable later.

Position that paper or electronic device so that you are ready to go.

Sometimes an empath will feel a bit shy about doing a new technique and scatter energy at a critical time by slowly opening up a notebook, searching for the right page, taking out the prettiest purple pen, using excellent calligraphy skills, etc.

Don't do that to yourself. Be prepared, then trust yourself enough to be sloppy, okay?

A HISTORIC MOMENT

Now you're oh-so-fully prepared for your first depth experience of Skilled Empath Merge. Let's pause briefly to consider this historic moment in your life.

Do you remember our definition of what it means to be an empath? An empath has at least one significant, trainable gift for directly experiencing what it is like to be another person.

Now you are finally about to use that ability. On purpose. And in a way where you are protected from picking up STUFF. Before our 30-Day Plan, you did plenty of unskilled Empath Merges, not nearly the same thing as using your talent on purpose.

Instead you did little bits, not-quite-consciously, here and there. Playing with your Space Dial has shown you how to consciously use your gift(s) better, but even a 10 on that dial delivers about 5% of the oomph of a dedicated Skilled Empath Merge.

Yes, you read that right. What you're about to do is a unique use of your gifts in life.

WORRIED?

What if you possess only one gift as an empath, and it is not for merging with people but with animals, plants, crystals or machines? That's Meg's plight, since her big talent is for being a Plant Empath.

Before doing Magic Picture, she's worrying. The guy in her photograph looks as much like a turnip as possible, but he's still not the same thing as a vegetable.

"What will become of me? Nothing?" she wails.

Fear not, Meg. Other highly specialized empaths, don't you worry one bit either. Although today's technique uses a human photo, the process of doing a Skilled Empath Merge will open up and direct your full talent. Tomorrow you will learn The Master Technique for Empath Merge, which you can adapt for use on any animal, plant, crystal or machine.

THROUGH, NOT WITH

Here's a secret about *all* techniques for Skilled Empath Merge. After you prepare properly, you will purposely switch ON the experience through one of your human senses.

"Through" is different from "with."

The experience does not depend on a sensation you would have directly *with* your hand or eye or ear. Instead, consciousness flows *through* one of your senses.

So don't expect a physical experience. Instead, accept an experience of consciousness where truth flows through, or by means of, your physical body.

Because you're human, one of your senses will always be involved in a technique for Skilled Empath Merge.

You're sure to have favorites among those senses, so that once you learn a range of techniques, you'll be able to identify the technique you like best. Long term, all you need is one. Other techniques can be used occasionally just to bring variety.

Magic Picture is a touchy-feely technique. Tomorrow you'll learn one that combines seeing with touch and has a huge array of variations. In the companion book *Empowered by Empathy,* you can find techniques for Skilled Empath Merge that involve hearing and taste, plus more that involve sight and touch.

Now let's roll up our sleeves and prepare for flow through!

THE YIN AND YANG OF HANDS

Doing Magic Picture, you will use one hand as a research tool. Which one?

Interlace your fingers. One of those thumbs will be on top.

If you're a rebel, like Meg, and could naturally put either thumb on top, congratulations. Now we know you're special. Can you still, please, choose one thumb to put on top?

Raise the hand attached to that thumb. This is your dominant hand. If you like, from now on you can call this hand "Mr. Yang." He's great for sending out healing energy.

Doing an Empath Merge isn't about sending healing energy, however. For this exercise, Mr. Yang will show his prowess simply by holding up your photo.

So raise your other hand. Meet "Ms. Yin," the hand with more feminine energy.

Keep track of which hand is which. It matters for all techniques of Skilled Empath Merge that involve touch.

"WAD" POSITION

Doing the Magic Picture technique, you'll hold Ms. Yin in a particular position which I call "Wad." Let's practice.

- Extend your thumb and all your fingers out straight. (You could consider this the opposite of making a fist.)
- Cupping your hand slightly, all five digits will be together.

Research Positions

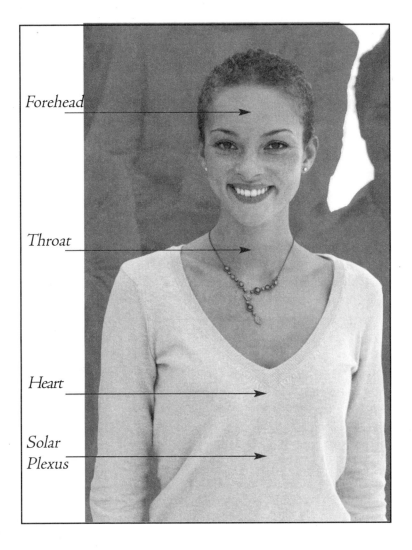

- Hold that hand up and look between the fingers. If you're
  doing Wad properly, you won't see space but, instead, a nice
  soft line where one finger makes contact with another. Even
  your thumb tip does something similar, lying against the
  base of your index finger.

About this cupped hand, is it held rigidly, causing pain? No, that would
be a different technique. Personally, I'm not into that technique. This
technique is for making an easy, comfortable, useful Wad.

RESEARCH POSITIONS

Magic Picture enables you to research a person from the inside out.
Four locations are especially interesting for doing this research, so I
call them "Research Positions."

Each position is centered at a particular body part:

- The forehead
- The throat
- The chest
- The ribcage

See our illustration on the previous page. Ours features beautiful Lexi.

Don't feel shy about staring at Lexi or anyone else. Don't think
you must be super-precise, either. You're aiming your hand for an
Empath Merge, not doing brain surgery.

These four Research Positions will aim your consciousness at
certain chakras, entry points into a person's aura. When that chosen
direction is combined with the rest of a particular technique, your
consciousness will have liftoff.

PRACTICING RESEARCH POSITIONS

Before we actually do this technique, let's do one final practice. Re-
hearsing these physical positions, don't be concerned with energy flows
or subjective anything. We're just getting you familiar with where to
place Ms. Yin, using Wad Position.

1. Using Mr. Yang, hold your photo up to eye level.
2. Hold Ms. Yin sideways, in Wad Position, a couple of inches away from the photo (or the screen containing the photo). Aim your palm at the person's forehead. You're your fingers point toward the right or left? Experiment and choose whichever angle is more comfortable. This is what we will call "Research Position at the Forehead."
3. Move that hand down a bit until you find "Research Position at the Throat."
4. Next, move down to "Research Position at Heart Level." That would be in the center of the body, at the breastbone.
5. Finally, move down to "Research Position at the Ribcage." It's in the center of the body, about halfway between the waist and the heart-level position you just practiced.

Now all our preparation is complete. Excellent!

Magic Picture

Here comes your Skilled Empath Merge. Read through the following instructions. Then go back and do them step by step, peeking at the words as needed.

1. Bring out the most important ingredient for this recipe: You. Sit comfortably, back erect, head not supported. Close your eyes and notice what it feels like to be you. That could be anything about your mind-body-spirit-intellect-soul-emotions-environment.
2. Paying attention to yourself is effortless but real. To make sure you've really made contact, shift your consciousness to a *second* category of your mind-body-spirit-intellect-soul-emotions-environment.
3. Get Big. Think the name "God," or another name you'd prefer, so long as it's your highest source of inspiration. (One quick thought does it. You're connected.)

4. Take a deep breath, settling into this subtly expanded version of being yourself.

5. Set an intention, such as "I'm ready to gain more wisdom." Think the thought once and consider the job done. You have directed your consciousness perfectly.

6. Hold up your Magic Picture with Mr. Yang. Move Ms. Yin into Research Position at the Forehead. Think this question: "What can I learn from this person about connecting to God?"

7. Immediately close your eyes and take a slow, deep breath. Take another. Then return to normal breathing.

8. Whatever you are experiencing now, in any way, is about your research subject. Open your eyes just enough to record your impressions on your notebook (or whatever). Remember, whatever you experience now *counts*, so make a quick note.

9. Move to Research Position at the Throat. Think this question: "Which strengths does this person bring to communicating in close relationships?" Repeat Steps 7-8.

10. Half-time break! Put your picture down. Stretch. Repeat Steps 1-5.

11. Move to Research Position at the Heart. Think this question: "Which strengths does this person bring to emotional connection to others?" Repeat Steps 7-8.

12. Move to Research Position at the Solar Plexus. Ask, "What is a gift of this person's soul for using power?" Repeat Steps 7-8.

13. Inwardly, say something like, "Thank you. Now this technique is over."

14. Return to the experience of being you. Notice at least two things about your mind-body-spirit-intellect-soul-emotions-environment.

15. Open your eyes. Consider your empath gift(s) officially turned OFF and rejoin your environment as The Most Important Person in The Room.

Done! Applause! What's the sound of one hand clapping, depending on whether it's Mr. Yang or Ms. Yin? Figuring that out is a different technique.

Seriously, this Skilled Empath Merge is officially over.

You can do the technique again whenever you like. But either you're doing it or you're not. And, right now, please, not!

Get in the habit of making a clear distinction. Over the past month, you've worked very hard to learn how to turn your gift(s) OFF. Now you're going back to OFF.

Feel the difference? Keep that distinction clear at every level of your being. *Either you're doing a technique to turn your gift(s) ON or else you're turning all those gift(s) OFF.*

The Magic Picture technique is like any dedicated technique for Skilled Empath Merge. It's spiritually powerful. The experience is more powerful than it might seem to a beginner. So is the quality of information received while those circuits are ON.

SWEET SUCCESS

Let's reflect on what you just accomplished. Otherwise you might miss it. That would not be because nothing happened but because what happened was so subtle. Skilled Empath Merges are done with consciousness.

Movies spoil us, with their big budgets and special effects. By contrast, Skilled Empath Merges are screened within you. That means all natural, deep as can be, but not flashy.

Pick up the notes you made and consider them. Reviewing your notes, start from this assumption: *I am magnificently talented at doing Empath Merges. And I just did something awesome.* Therefore:

- No need to be a harsh critic.
- Forget about doubting your experiences: The way this technique was set up, everything counted.
- Never repeat research that you have already done. Throat research on Mr. Turnip Face can be considered complete! Hey, only a zillion other photos in the world remain for you to research.

- Remember, the only way to have more vivid experiences in the future is to be grateful for what you receive now. In more innocent days, when you first learned to read, you did this gratitude thing pretty darned well, remember?

EVERYTHING COUNTS

Once I gave a workshop for empaths where students were paired up to do Empath Merges. After doing the technique, Barbie was upset. She told pulled me over to complain:

"It was just awful. Not only did nothing happen when I did your technique, but I felt fat and blobby, like I weighed a hundred extra pounds.

"All of a sudden, for no reason at all, just being in the workshop made me nervous, as if I had social anxiety or something weird like that.

"And I don't mean to brag, but usually people call me intelligent. Doing your technique, my mind became dull. Really, I don't think I have ever felt so fat. And blobby. And stupid."

Oh, the tact needed! Have you guessed? Barbie was giving a great description about how it felt temporarily experiencing what it was like to be her partner.

So I'm not kidding. Once you get to Step 8 of Magic Picture, everything counts. Usually your experiences will be positive and fascinating, but not always. Don't let your Empath Merge sneak up on you.

YOUR ASSIGNMENT FOR DAY 28

Your optional assignment for today is to do Magic Picture once more, only researching a different picture.

Use the same four Research Positions. But you can choose different questions to ask, if you like. Experiment.

One source of ideas is *Read People Deeper,* also by me and published by Women's Intuition Worldwide, LLC. It's a whole book dedicated to researching practical aspects of life, like how people deal with money, communication, sex, honesty. Many chakra databanks are included. And you'll find two versions of Magic Picture, one for sight plus the one for touch.

Both are presented as techniques for aura reading. But here's a secret I wish all empaths knew.

Know This Secret?

Before you do *any* technique for aura reading, you had better learn to become a Skilled Empath. Otherwise you're going to do Empath Merges every single time you try to read auras.

So you would be wise to consider that every experience you have while doing a dedicated technique to read auras does count. It's just the same as if you were doing a dedicated technique for Empath Merge.

But will you be protected against taking on other people's STUFF? Not necessarily. That depends on the technique being used.

Our Magic Picture technique, like the technique you'll learn tomorrow, has been designed to shape a full and balanced experience for you, protection included.

Some of you Brave Explorers are very sophisticated about aura reading already, while others of you are new to it.

Newbies, you're really fortunate to have begun with Empath Empowerment. I've taught aura reading to thousands of students, and a very high proportion have been unskilled empaths. Today, many healers and psychics don't yet realize that Empath Empowerment is a smart prerequisite if they aim to study aura reading, Reiki, Emotional Freedom Technique, hypnosis, psychotherapy, psychic development, etc.

If you *are* an experienced aura reader, you can adapt other aura reading techniques into safe, Skilled Empath Merge techniques. Just be sure to include Steps 1-5 and 13-15 of Magic Picture. This will protect you and, simultaneously, help to deepen your experience.

Whichever techniques you use for Skilled Empath Merge, remember this. Either do the technique or don't. A very small amount of conscious Empath Merge goes a very long way, so remember to keep your lifestyle in balance.

During the rest of today, do just one more research session, tops, using Magic Picture. Otherwise, use all the skills you've developed to keep your gifts nicely turned OFF.

Day 29. The Master Technique

Fat and blobby, tall and perky, or giggly and silly and wise — how did you wind up feeling when you did your homework yesterday? Doing your first full-blown technique for Skilled Empath Merge, you began to jet-propel yourself into the experience of Otherness.

Never will you be able to anticipate how another person's Otherness will be. The experience is always unique. It differs completely from using emotional intelligence, expression reading, or other superficial approaches. Remember Day 23, when we discussed deep vs. shallow?

Exploring someone's façade is another popular ways to learn what someone is really like; for an empath it's right at the shallow end of the swimming pool. A *façade* is a personality projection, how a person tries to appear in public. In every social relationship, each party wears a façade.

Hairstyle, makeup, etc. can add impact to a façade. Personally, I think it's sad when people get better clothes or a "makeover" and then proclaim, "I'm a new person." Sure, it's true... if that person is so shallow that inner experience goes no deeper than façade. Today's vanity culture is all about conflating the surface of life into "all that is." But you are daring to be counter-culture, seeking truth all the way to its innermost parts.

Otherness means the direct experience of what makes a person distinctive. Whenever you do a technique for Skilled Empath Merge, your consciousness goes as deep as can be, moving way beyond surface projections like façade. You wake up to find yourself *inside* the person's reality, experiencing Otherness.

Want a hilarious new hobby? Try doing MagicPicture with a photo where the model is supposedly meditating, sleeping, kissing or enjoying the taste of food. The model's inner experience while posing is sure to be different. Attention is more likely devoted to personal matters, like "Does my chest look good?"

Bam! Courtesy of a Skilled Empath Merge, you have tweaked an illusion. It's like Zachary snapping his suspenders. Notice the rich twanging sound.

Transcending the efforts people make to "think outside the box," you can travel there. Usually, people live inside their own boxes. Even an empath like Zachary lives inside his own box. Trying to *think* outside your own box is a noble but two-dimensional experience, like drawing a line. *Moving* outside your own box, doing a Skilled Empath Merge into another person's box, brings you Otherness. Consider that a fifth-dimensional experience.

- You receive the full three dimensions of human experience, what it is like to be that other person.
- You do this moving through time, the fourth dimension.
- Doing a Skilled Empath Merge, you are touching down inside that other person's consciousness, moving within it as you might move inside your physical body.
- This quality of having consciousness be your prime mover in life (Wow!) means having experience at the fifth dimension.

So much for theory. How about practice? Let's say that you do a Skilled Empath Merge with Zachary. You might notice characteristics like these:

- Physically, his face feels tight around the mouth, and he has this cute default expression of sneering.
- Emotionally, he appears cut off from people. Actually, Zachary goes through more emotions than an outsider might guess. And he does have Emotional Oneness.
- Intellectually, Zachary is quite exhausted right now. Who wouldn't be, favoring his emotions constantly, then using his intellect to try to calm all those feelings down?
- What's Zachary's biggest secret? He loves insects. Gotta love a man who has spent much of his life doing

spontaneous, unskilled Empath Merges with ants. Talented as an Animal Empath, he happens to specialize in insects. Golly, before starting our 30-Day Plan, perhaps you thought *you* had been doing a thankless form of volunteer work!

ABOUT THAT VOLUNTEER WORK

Whenever you do an Empath Merge, skilled or not, it's volunteer work. Before I teach you the Master Technique for doing Skilled Empath Merges at will, let's consider that. Fun aside, what's the point of doing volunteer work as a Skilled Empath?

As a Skilled Empath, you can turn your gift(s) ON for *service.* Say that you're a psychotherapist (officially or unofficially). You might do one Skilled Empath Merge with your "client" right at the start of your conversation. After that, go back to being yourself. Use your regular skill set for helping that person. That skill set might include:

- Your working knowledge of psychology, helping people to find their own way.
- The sensitive use of advice and wisdom from others, given your discernment as The Most Important Person in the Room.
- Reiki or other healing methods you have learned from workshops
- 12 Steps to Cut Cords of Attachment®, which you could have learned from me

Such a long list of skills you have available! And now, of course, your list includes keeping your empath gift(s) nicely turned OFF most of the time, Space Dial set at 1, using the "Take It" technique, etc.

Service done in this way will be far more effective than service done in personal burnout mode, Space Dial at 10, heaping STUFF from others into your already STUFF-packed aura.

Living as a Skilled Empath, you'll find many practical uses... high-functioning uses... for the amazingly deep gift(s) you have had your whole life. This is especially true when you add the ability to do Skilled Empath Merges.

Many more people know about autism than about being wired as an empath. Experts may call a particular autistic child "high-functioning" because that child is able to adapt well to life among those who aren't autistic.

Empaths, too, can be high-functioning. Only the concept of high- or low-functioning relates to exceptional abilities rather than an illness. Unskilled empaths are low-functioning, since each empath gift become a basis for suffering. Unskilled empaths appear to function normally as human beings but they're not using their capacity to safely and clearly experience Otherness.

During our 30-Day Plan, you have learned to become The Most Important Person in the Room, turning your empath gift(s) OFF. This makes you a moderately-functioning empath. Only when you gain skill at turning your empath gift(s) ON, as part of a balanced life, do you become a truly high-functioning empath. Then your contribution to life can become extraordinary.

BE A HIGH-FUNCTIONING EMPATH

Society today has almost zero understanding of what it means to be a high-functioning empath, what we have been calling all along a fully "Skilled Empath," someone who does Skilled Empath Merges at will.

You are becoming that new kind of person, which prepares you for remarkable service to humanity.

- *Service* to others as a high-functioning empath is like having someone you really respect (Archangel Raphael? George Clooney? God?) whisper the most important secrets about your "client." Then you proceed to do service based on that deepest possible knowledge.
- As a high-functioning empath, turning your gift(s) ON greatly deepens your *wisdom*. At will, you can plunge into the direct experience of Otherness, a completely different way to be. Think, feel, and be inside the box — somebody else's box.
- Remember the example of doing an Empath Merge with a model in some silly ad? That can *smash spiritual illusions*

for you in a way that is not inferior to Buddha's process beneath his famed banyan tree.

- Or you could merge with a photo of *your biggest hero.* Talk about inspiration!
- Do you have someone in your life whom you have tried to *forgive* but just can't? A Skilled Empath Merge might help.
- Opening up *the heart of compassion* – that's my fancy name for the soul wisdom you gain every time that you choose to do a Skilled Empath Merge.
- How about doing the Magic Picture technique on a photo of yourself 10 years ago? It's no science-fiction time travel. Instead, use this real and very practical way to *understand yourself* with uncanny accuracy. And the better you know yourself, as a high-functioning empath, the greater your reach when giving service to others.

Today you'll expand your service as a high-functioning empath by learning my Master Technique for Empath Merge. As with learning Magic Picture, we'll start by practicing different aspects of physical position.

YOUR LATEST RESEARCH TOOL

Eyes are about to become your latest tool for Skilled Empath Merge For our Master Technique, you will look at one particular body part at a time, the visual equivalent of what you did yesterday when putting your hand into Research Position. Using eyes, you will have one major DO and several important DON'Ts.

DO aim your eyes at one body part at a time. On the following page, there's an illustration of Cute Guy researching Gail's forehead, so we'll use her as an example.During Empath Merge,

DON'T use your eyes for any of these other purposes:

- Deciding if you like Gail's clothes, jewelry and makeup.
- Evaluating if Gail is good or nice or not.
- Reading Gail's mood from facial expression and posture.

Aim Your Eyes for Research

Doing a technique for Skilled Empath Merge, choose one Research Position at a time. Here Cute Guy is aiming at Gail's forehead.

- Trying to guess how Gail thinks, feels, etc.
- Assessing Gail's sex appeal.
- Squinting, trying to make Gail look more like a turnip.

MORE ABOUT AIMING YOUR EYES

Doing the Master Technique, you'll use your eyes to connect up to the other person. The following technique-within-a-technique will help you to take a break, whether in advance of doing Skilled Empath Merge, during the merge or afterwards.

Refresh Your Inner Screen

Use this simple technique to gain clarity, like when you're reading online and seek freshly updated information.

1. Close your eyes.
2. Take a deep breath.
3. Think this intention once: "I'm ready to receive the full truth of my experience, here and now."
4. Take another deep breath and know that you have been given a fresh new start.
5. Open your eyes.

Refresh Your Inner Screen at the beginning of a technique, at the end, or in the middle. Do it whenever you want a fresh start for using your eyes in an Empath Merge technique.

SAFELY MERGE AT WILL

This super-flexible Master Technique should be done with a real, live person in the room with you. Let's call this person "Lexi." (See her on Page 207 for a reminder of Research Positions.)

And now comes the rest of your preparation.

The Master Technique will add two additional Research Positions to your repertoire, belly and leg. For "belly," choose any spot on the abdominal area. For "leg," choose either leg and then pick one spot on that leg. To brush up on which hand is "Ms. Yin," see Page 206. You'll be using Wad Position, so you might also want to refresh your understanding of that, too (Page 206-208).

Use common sense, of course, in choosing your research subject. Avoid doing Empath Merge with any person who is obviously crazy, angry, high on drugs, etc. Otherwise you might have to take a lot of showers afterwards! Also, do Empath Merge on just one person at a time. (If you don't understand why, go back and re-do Day 26.)

To use your gift as a Plant Empath, Crystal Empath, Environmental Empath, etc., your research subject "Lexi" could be a plant, crystal, etc. You could even go hiking in your favorite landscape and have the environment be your "Lexi."

Master Technique for Skilled Empath Merge

1. Close your eyes and notice at least two different things about yourself right now. Choose from categories of your mind-body-spirit-intellect-soul-emotions-environment.

2. Get Big. Think the name "God," or another name that you'd prefer as your highest source of inspiration. (One quick thought does it. You're connected.)

3. Set an intention, e.g., Think, "I choose to gain greater wisdom."

4. Jump-start a Skilled Empath Merge through one of these methods, always using Ms. Yin in Wad Position.

• Look at Lexi. Think, "When I touch my heart, this will jet-propel me inside Lexi's heart." Then place Ms. Yin palm down in the center of your chest and take a deep breath.

• Look at Lexi. Think, "When I touch my ribcage, this will jet-propel me inside Lexi's mind and intellect." Then place Ms. Yin palm down in the center of your front ribcage and take a deep breath.

• Look at Lexi. Think, "When I touch my belly, this will jet-propel me inside Lexi's gut." Then place Ms. Yin palm down in the center of your belly and take a deep breath.

• Look at Lexi. Think, "When I touch my leg, this will jet-propel me inside Lexi's body." Then place Ms. Yin palm down on one of your thighs and take a deep breath.

• If "Lexi" is an animal, plant, crystal or machine, place Ms. Yin palm down on any part of your body you favor and know that you are connected. So take a deep breath and know that you'll be learning the most important info. available to you from that particular "Lexi."

5. Everything that happens next counts as information about Lexi. Close your eyes to intensify your experience. Breathe deeply to turn up the volume of your inner knowing.

6. Staying connected, ask one question at a time about what is going on with Lexi. Be sure to include a positive question like, "What can I learn about [Name one aspect of life, such as "Spiritual Connection" or "Physical Coordination"] from Lexi?"

7. After asking each question, just be. Stay connected. Breathe. Count everything that happens to you now as valid information. Yes, that means any experience you are having about your mind-body-spirit-intellect-soul-emotions-environment.

8. Move your hand. Release the connection.

9. Make quick notes about what you have learned. Ideally, write them down or make a sound recording. Even if you're not doing "ideal," make the best mental notes you can.

10. Close your eyes. Inwardly say, "God (or your choice of Divine Being), cut all psychic ties between myself and Lexi. Fill each of us with your love and light, power and peace."

11. Conclude with something like, "Thank you. Now this technique is over."

12. Return to the experience of being you. Notice at least two things about your mind-body-spirit-intellect-soul-emotions-environment. Consider your empath gift(s) officially turned OFF and rejoin your environment as The Most Important Person in The Room.

The more you practice Skilled Empath Merge, the better you'll get at it. Or, more precisely, you'll gain trust. That includes trusting that you know what you know. Although practice will help you, remember to practice in moderation. During our 30-Day Plan you've worked hard to get your life in balance. Keep that balance, even if sometimes you must issue the equivalent of a restraining order.

RESTRAINING ORDER

Recently, I did a session to help Genevieve, a client with a rather special relationship to a man I'll call "Buddy." Genevieve knew him for one week in high school. Fast forward a mere 15 years and Buddy had begun stalking her. In Buddy's twisted mind, Genevieve had become "his love."

Buddy hasn't stalked Genevieve lately. But only because he's in jail. Imagine being Genevieve, getting a call from the penitentiary. (This conversation really did happen.) "Buddy is calling to request a conjugal visit."

She said, "I'm not married to Buddy. I never even dated him."

"Does that mean you don't want to give him a conjugal visit?"

"You got that right."

> "Buddy wants you to know, he won't hurt you. All he wants to do is hold you like a puppy."
> Is Earth School an amazing place or what?

Genevieve is doing fine now, thank you. I mention her story here is that most empaths could use a restraining order. Not against Buddy, thank God. But we need to restrain our gift(s) as empaths.

Remember to keep balanced. That's your priority, no matter how much you love doing Empath Merges. Allow yourself to be The Most Important Person in The Room. And let's be clear. Your reason to feel important is *not* because you have the power to move in and out of other people's experiences but because mostly you're just being you.

A person could get carried away with this new toy. Skilled Empath Merges bring powerful shifts of experience, exploration of Otherness that would make any true science fiction buff want to drool with envy. You may be tempted to overdo.

But don't. Commit to staying balanced as a person. For the best possible quality of life, keep using all the skills developed during our previous days, and add just a wee bit of Empath Merge.

Most days, *just a short time* is plenty. One 30-minute practice period per day, max, for the rest of our 30-Days — and for the next 30, too. That's ideal for adding Skilled Empath Merge to your lifestyle.

In everyday situations, notice when you are becoming involved in someone else's story or energies. Are you going to make *this* the time you experiment? Does another person's pressure create *your* emergency? Skilled Empath Merges aren't terribly different from conjugal visits, minus the commute time. Choose your partner wisely.

Once you agree to this, you can safely make The Master Technique a part of your daily life.

YOUR ASSIGNMENT FOR DAY 29

No homework is needed. But you might want to play with The Master Technique, just for the fun of it. Or do Magic Picture again, for exercising different empath's muscles, and then return to today's technique. All this would be for 30 minutes maximum, remember? Then return to being The Most Important Person in The Room.

Day 30. Completion

After a Skilled Empath Merge, even Roscoe seems like a knight in shining armor. He may not be *your* knight in shining armor. But you can purposely move in and out of the experience of being him, which offers definite potential for experiencing Otherness. Magnificent!

Brave Explorer, you have learned techniques for sampling magnificent Otherness, either in person or via photo. However well you have done so far, your clarity will only improve over time.

Gaining access to a desired experience whenever you like — that's one reason to use techniques. You don't have to wait until you haphazardly slip-and-slide into an experience of Otherness. Moreover you can do a strong Skilled Empath Merge *safely* now, without picking up anyone else's STUFF.

Of course, you're doing Skilled Empath Merge for reasonable amounts of time and always for a purpose, correct?

And otherwise you're concentrating on being yourself, right?

I sure hope so, because that combo is the essence of being a Skilled Empath, high-functioning, having the most wonderful life. Today you complete our 30-Day Plan. Let's summarize what you have learned.

---

10 Ways to Be a Skilled Empath

1. Mostly you keep your empath gift(s) turned OFF.
2. You do this in a natural way that wakes you up from inside, without a speck of phony or manipulative *anything*.
3. To help other people in social situations, you use a variety of normal skill sets — just as non-empaths do. These skills

could include assertiveness, striving to balance give-and-take in relationships, taking effective action in the outer world.

4. Gone is the old habit of assuming that helping people automatically means that you connect with them energetically and take on their STUFF.

5. Gone is the old habit of being over-subjective. When something in objective life becomes a problem, you take action in the objective realm.

6. You understand that Empath Empowerment involves *subtle* shifts in how you use consciousness. Easy does it, no big effort required.

7. But should effort be required to help someone else, that's when to use the "Take It" technique, so you never have to play God while in a human body.

8. Now, when you turn your empath gift(s) ON, you're making it a quality experience.

9. By playing with the combination of OFF and ON in your day, and sprinkling in plenty of grounding, you have developed balance in your life.

10. Ta da! Wherever you go, you are now The Most Important Person in The Room. Enjoy your new status. Do you find it tasty? Terrific? Positively twinkling?

Oh, I have so many questions for you. Let's turn them into an official quiz..

GRADUATION QUIZ

When you answer the following questions, feel free to brag.

1. Thanks to Empath Empowerment, you've got more of a life now. Has anyone noticed a change in you? Have you?

2. As of today, which are your favorite categories of mind-body-spirit-intellect-soul-emotions-environment?

3. Does any of those *MBS. I see!* categories still need a little more quality attention, such as dedicated time each day or, even, healing? (No shame in that, remember.)

4. Yesterday, how many times did you use The Wakeup Affirmation? Could you have been more generous with it, using it more often?

5. When was the last time you did Advanced Bingo, and what happened?

6. As a Skilled Empath, are you looking at people differently now? I mean that literally, as in our Eye Muscles technique.

7. Are you satisfied with the décor in your Room of Requirement? (You can always change it, you know.)

8. Think of a tricky ongoing relationship, one that used to be draining. How are you using your Space Dial now with this person? As a consequence, what has shifted?

9. Guilt: Comparing now to 30 days ago, do you have more guilt or less?

10. "What I do isn't enough." Comparing now to 30 days ago, do you have more of that old worry or less?

11. Your nose. Compared to 30 days ago, do you have more nose or less? (Okay, I'm kidding about that part. But this Question 11 is a great place to write about anything else you consider important about your growth as an empath.)

12. What is still a growth area — or relationship — for you?

You have a lot to be proud of, don't you! For a skilled empath, stories about your personal growth trickle in. And you want it that way, not change with all the subtlety of Niagara Falls. Trust me on this one.

MAGNIFICENCE

Every human being alive is, in some way, magnificent. If you weren't an empath, you might have to settle for theory about this.

I host a blog called "Deeper Perception Made Practical." Recently Kudzu, a poetic young man, wrote this comment:

> more and more I try to see others as sources of spiritual light
> in the firmament.
> I try to see people as soft blue glows all around me
> gratitude and humility

Kudzu has neatly summarized three different techniques. There are innumerable techniques for imagining a better experience of reality and to strive for a more spiritual connection to others. When I first read Kudzu's words, I could feel his tremendous yearning for more in life.

Sweet! But let's bring some discernment to balance the admiration. From your perspective as a Skilled Empath, what is limiting about Kudzu's techniques?

You may find it useful to distinguish techniques made from *within* your own box (like Kudzu's) to techniques about moving into another person's box entirely.

Empath Merges are the ultimate way to move into another person's box. But what if, like Kudzu, someone is not an empath? I teach techniques of Deeper Perception that anyone can do successfully:

- You have already played with my highly counter-culture approach to body language. Depending on whether you are an empath or not, body language can be shallow or deep.
- Face Reading Secrets® is a skill set that can be used (in person or through photos) to go outside your box and see each person's face as meaningful, highly informative, even sacred.
- Aura Reading Through All Your Senses® is another outside-the-box skill set. It can be used in person or

through photos, revealing subtle truths that cannot be faked.

- 12 Steps to Cut Cords of Attachment® is a skill set to improve the quality of what's inside *your* box. Specifically, you can surgically remove forms of STUFF that have become embedded in your aura and subconscious mind, replaying 24/7.

What happens when an empath like you uses any form of Deeper Perception to understand the dynamics of another person's box? Watch out! Whoa! You're probably going to switch ON your gift(s) as an empath.

That's right. Even if Empath Merge isn't part of the official job description, you'll probably do it. The same goes for skills like Emotional Freedom Technique (E.F.T.), Reiki healing, Energy Medicine, hypnosis, massage, teaching, nursing, being a really good receptionist.

Automatic empathic travel will happen to you, even if it isn't officially taught in these different skill sets. This point was touched on before in the context of studying aura reading. But let's expand this point here, since today is Completion Day.

Unless you purposely turn your gifts OFF, you'll do unskilled Empath Merges while you give, *or receive,* any intuitive skill, service occupation, healing modality. Be aware of that. Just because you can now do Skilled Empath Merges doesn't mean that you'll never do the unskilled kind again.

So remember to use the Turn-OFF techniques you have learned throughout our 30-Day Plan.

Use them especially in conjunction with any skill set that might otherwise trigger an Empath Merge. In addition, as a smart precaution, here is the final technique in our 30-Day Plan.

Help Others WITHOUT Empath Merge

Before you start that job or work on that client:

1. Close your eyes and notice at least two different things about your about your mind-body-spirit-intellect-soul-emotions-environment.

2. Get Big. Think the name "God," or another name that you would rather use to call on your highest source of inspiration. (One quick thought does it. You're connected.)

3. Set an intention, e.g., "I choose to be of service to Lexi."

4. Use the skill set that does not require that you be an empath, e.g., Reiki, Energy Medicine, E.F.T., Cut Cords of Attachment.

5. After you finish, say, "God (or your choice of Divine Being), cut and dissolve all psychic ties between myself and this person. Fill each of us with your love and light, power and peace. We are free to accept as much of this as we wish."

6. Inwardly, say something like, "Thank you. This technique is now over."

7. Return to the experience of being you and notice at least two things about your mind-body-spirit-intellect-soul-emotions-environment.

8. Consider your empath gift(s) officially turned OFF and rejoin your environment as The Most Important Person in The Room.

Remember that results of Skilled Empath Merge are subtle. When you have done several, you'll begin to notice contrast. With time and more experience, contrast will become more refined still. You'll move in and out, being other people temporarily, using consciousness to become aware of true Otherness.

PEEK AT YOUR FUTURE

Being a Skilled Empath means so much more than Becoming the Most Important Person in the Room. You are fortified against unwitting Empath Merges while doing other techniques. Altogether, you can confidently expect to play an exciting new role in life, showing the world how to live with Empath Empowerment.

Among the millions of unskilled empaths in the world, you can be a leader. Through your behavior, your knowledge, even on the level of your aura, you can serve as a role model for every empath you meet.

True spiritual lessons are caught, not taught. Living as a balanced, powerful empath, you're going to help innumerable people through your example.

Being The Most Important Person in The Room could be just the start of your new, improved way of living in the world.

But let's get personal. What will Empath Empowerment mean for *your* life, now and in the future? As we end our 30-Day Plan, here's one last daily assignment.

YOUR ASSIGNMENT FOR DAY 30

At random times today, dream a bit. Dream about the future you'd like to step into as a high-functioning, Skilled Empath.

Already you're living in balance, with growing awareness of your gift(s). How might all this skill mature by ten years from now? Here are my predictions.

1. You will be able to do Skilled Empath Merges at will. Safely!
2. You'll be strong enough to do them many times a day.
3. You'll know when it is wise to do them.
4. You'll also feel comfortable using that skill set very, very sparingly.
5. Everywhere you go, you'll feel like The Most Important Person in The Room.
6. Yet you can freely appreciate how others also feel like The Most Important Person in The Room. You'll be able to serve them and learn from them with all due respect.
7. Each day that you live on earth, you'll develop greater appreciation for who you are as a person and also for Otherness.

How open can your heart be? Could you spontaneously stop judging people because you find such magnificence in them? Will your Skilled Empath Merges gradually take on a quality of sacredness?

Dressed in your glorious human identity, living inside your own box, how graceful and glorious can that human life of yours become?

Besides leaving you with these questions, I'd like to offer you this final bit of advice.

Skilled Empath Merging with people, by choice, is always a high. Yet it can be compared to eating ice cream and candy.

Treat yourself. Consider it your reward for attending that tough place I call "Earth School." Maybe even think of it like eating a communion wafer.

But also eat your vegetables, okay?

Index

Q

Questions 68, 151-153, 156, 178-179, 180-181, 195, 212
Quiz 7-15, 18, 127-130, 131, 158-159, 226

R

Regression therapy 63, 190
Reiki vii, 119, 213, 217, 229, 230
Religion iii, 12-13, 71, 81, 84, 149-150
Research Positions 207, 221
Resistance 60-63, 79, 117-125, 153, 188, 190-191
Room of Requirement 197-200, 227

S

Sacrifice 148, 149
Sadness (*Also see* STUFF.) iv, 10, 78, 84-85, 93, 97
Self-awareness 5, 56, **95**, 158, 187-188, 191, 218
Self-confidence 5, 82, 95, 147
Self-talk 149, **177-181**
Selfishness xiii, 12, 59, 128, 141, 159
Service to others 19, 35, 52, 54, 66, 73, 148, 203, 218, 225, 230
Sex 3, 10, **96,** 137, 138-139, 175, 183, 220
Shards of time **25-26,** 33, 34
Shields *See* Boundaries and Walls.
Shifts of Consciousness 12, 27, 41, 51, 57, 65, 69, 73, 79, 80, 92, 98, 100, 111, 114, 157, 174, 187, 197, 208
Skill sets 14, 60, 73, 74, 78, 98, 150, 167, 194, 217, 228, 229, 231
Skilled Empath iv, 12, 28, 41, 58, 94-96, 148, 154, 171, 194, 213
Skilled Empath Merge 73, 183, **201-213**, 215-224, 229, 231, 232
Smothering 155, 159
Soul 60, 65, 77, 84, **87-90**, 91-96, 190, 196, 218
Soul Thrill 89, 120, 121, 123, 124
Space Dial **133-146,** 163, 165, 167, 169-171, 173, 174, 181, 205, 217, 227
Spirit 60, 65, 77, 78, **81-86**, 87-88, 91-96, 120, 121, 122-124
Spiritual Intuition 12
Spiritual Oneness **13,** 163

Books for Empaths

*All these titles by Rose Rosetree are published by
Women's Intuition Worldwide, LLC.*

Empowered by Empathy

This was the first how-to book for empaths in the English language.
It shows how to use spiritual awareness to turn inborn gifts OFF or
ON at will. This contrasts with more common approaches, behavior
based, such as "strengthen your boundaries." Many techniques are presented for safely doing a Skilled Empath Merge.

Empowered by Empathy, The Audiobook

Classical radio broadcaster Marilyn Cooley joins Rose in reading the
pioneering how-to book for empaths. Especially recommended for
those who learn well by listening, the skill sets in this book carry the
extra oomph of being read by Skilled Empaths. This CD set includes
over seven hours of personal instruction.

Read People Deeper

Empaths can use the techniques in this book to do Skilled Empath
Merges to answer practical questions about power style, truthfulness,
money, sex — 50 categories in all. Besides being the first how-to book
to combine body language + face reading + aura reading, this title
pioneers one of the most useful discoveries in the history of reading
auras, chakra databanks.

Cut Cords of Attachment

Use this book to become a better consumer of services offered for
spiritual healing. Or use Rosetree's 12 Steps to Cut Cords of Attach-

ment® to heal yourself and others. Psychotherapists, energy workers, and intuitives will appreciate the systematic presentation and detailed examples of "cord dialogue." This is the first how-to book about cutting cords in the English language.

Aura Reading Through All Your Senses

Here Rose pioneers her easy-to-learn method of Aura Reading Through All Your Senses®. Discover how aura reading can improve relationships, health, even your choices as a consumer. Whether you're a beginner or an experienced aura reader, this how-to will move you forward, with over 100 practical techniques. The German edition of this book became a national bestseller.

The Roar of the Huntids (A Novel for Empaths)

This spiritual thriller is a coming-of-age story about an unskilled empath, Rachel Murphy. Set in the year 2020, the story is spiced with social and political satire, plus a fast-moving plot, romance, and quirky characters (some of whom are empaths and some who are definitely not).

The Power of Face Reading

Rosetree has been called "The mother of American physiognomy." Her system of Face Reading Secrets® brings you soulful interpretations of physical face data, with nuanced but highly accurate readings about personal style — a useful addition to your skill set for reading people accurately without having to do full-blown Empath Merges.

Wrinkles Are God's Makeup: How You Can Find Meaning in Your Evolving Face

In the 5,000-year history of reading faces for character, this is the first to explore how faces change over time. Lavishly illustrated, the comparison photos help you to become a spiritual talent scout. A special section details psychological and spiritual problems linked to cosmetic surgery.

Let Today Be a Holiday: 365 Ways to Co-Create with God

Explore practical skills and ideas for balancing world service as an empath with being happy, effective and *human*.

Acknowledgments

Special thanks go to Anita Chu, M.D., the talented student and molecular empath who coined the term "Empath Merge."

(Molecular empaths are described in the companion book, *Empowered by Empathy*. Since you have read so far into this one, here comes an extra reward for you in the form of a key concept for your advanced study: Of course, there could be additional, rare empath gifts not covered in this or, so far, any book for empaths!)

Speaking of amazing empaths, I'm nearly inexpressibly grateful to my mentors for the past 20 years. Bill Bauman, Ph.D. has helped me to move out major STUFF and think bigger. Tantra Maat has used her multi-dimensional awareness to inspire me.

Both mentors have given me extra strength as needed for teaching new systems of Empath Empowerment, Aura Reading, Cutting Cords of Attachment, Face Reading, etc. (If you do Face Reading, check out my chin thrust. You'll appreciate what a stretch it has been for me, moving new knowledge into the world.)

Additional thanks go to AlixSandra Parness and TIC for introducing me to the concept of objective-subjective balance (and more).

Then come the more personal acknowledgments, starting with my husband, Mitch Weber.

My best friend for over 30 years, Mitch recognized the best in me even when I was a hugely STUFF-filled unskilled empath. He continues to support both my human life and my work as a World Server, adding the kind of support that only a really talented empath can give. What he doesn't know about service could fit in a thimble.

Our son, Matt Weber, was a pre-schooler during the ecstatic three months when I wrote the first draft of *Empowered by Empathy*. For the next 3 ½ years, I did the hard work of editing.

This was my first experience of receiving a big spiritual knowledge download, then making it intelligible to other human beings. If Matt hadn't been such an easy, delightful, inspiring child to raise, I might never have published that first book for empaths.

Then and through all the following years of writing, giving personal sessions and teaching workshops, Matt has been supportive of my work in every possible way, including his huge talent as an empath.

Now getting ready for college, Matt has silently added his consciousness to Mitch's and mine and that of the Divine Beings who joined with me as I wrote this book. They, of course, get all the biggest credit for this book and this knowledge.

And a special shout-out goes to understatedly amazing Julie Schroedl, Coordinator for my Intensive Workshops.

Finally, I want to thank every friend, reader, student, client and commenter at my blog (www.roserosetree.com/blog) where we have so many conversations around being a Skilled Empath.

You know who you are, so take a minute to feel deep down the value of your contribution and my gratitude. When people sincerely desire to know and grow, knowledge must flow.

Thank you so much, all you Brave Explorers. Together, may we add to humanity's collective knowledge of what it means to be a Skilled Empath. I have a hunch we're just getting started!

Advanced Studies
for a Skilled Empath

This book is designed to do the big job, turning you into a Skilled Empath. But what if you want to move forward faster than one day at a time? Unless you have a time machine, you might wish to avail yourself of the following resources. Every one of them can move your skills forward by three months or more:

1. ANOTHER RECOMMENDED BOOK FOR EMPATHS

Empowered by Empathy is my original how-to for empaths. It contains loads of new information about the nature of your gifts, why they work, and how to turn them OFF. In addition, there is the most detailed information you'll find anywhere for dedicated, safe techniques of Empath Merge to turn your gifts ON.

This book is the perfect supplement to what you have learned so far, deepening your understanding and experience. Be sure to do the technique for "Coming Home."

Editions available include audiobook, print, and e-book. Foreign editions, at the time of publishing *this* book, include Spanish, Japanese, and Turkish.

Browse the current collection of foreign editions off the home page at my website, www.rose-rosetree.com.

2. PERSONAL COACHING

Many developing empaths like to add that personal touch, coaching sessions where you benefit from my experience helping thousands of empaths directly and doing Skilled Empath Merge into YOU. I can answer your questions and coach you in ways that are custom-designed just for your current skill level.

Personal coaching can be done by phone, one session at a time. Or you can come to town for a full day of Coaching and Mentoring. Right now, I'm located in the suburbs of Washington, D.C.

- For research, browse my main website, www.rose-rosetree.com. (Look on the left for "Order Sessions.")
- Not into computers? No worries! Send a request for information along with a stamped, self-addressed envelope to Rose Rosetree, 116 Hillsdale Drive, Sterling, VA 20164-1201.
- When you have decided to make an appointment, send an email to rose@rose-rosetree.com or call 703-450-9514. We'll set you up.

3. HEALING AND TRANSFORMATION

With all you know now, there's nothing to keep you from becoming a Skilled Empath except for… STUFF. Depending on patterns stuck in your aura, it may be difficult for you to fully implement all the skills you've begun to explore in this book. That's why you might want to consider a session with me for Aura Healing and Transformation.

Mostly, these sessions are done by phone, but you can also come to my office. During a personal session, I can do an Empath Merge (Skilled!) and then use appropriate techniques from my other skill sets. Often it is helpful to cut a cord of attachment.

Cords of attachment are energy patterns between people that keep repeating 24/7, dumping toxic STUFF into a person's subconscious mind and aura.

For example, you may have a cord of attachment where patterns include your doing an unskilled Empath Merge with the person at the other end of the cord.

By permanently removing such a cord, that depth healing will help your skill-level take a giant leap forward. Otherwise, ongoing patterns of STUFF can make it unnecessarily difficult for you to use keep your empath gift(s) turned OFF.

Less STUFF in your aura also equals greater clarity when you do Skilled Empath Merges. If you wish to use your gifts in service to humanity, personal sessions can be an investiment in your helping others.

- To research personal sessions of healing, browse at www.rose-rosetree.com. (Look on the left for "Order Sessions" and "FAQs.")
- Or send an inquiry along with a stamped, self-addressed envelope to Rose Rosetree, 116 Hillsdale Drive, Sterling, VA 20164-1201.
- When you have decided to make an appointment, send an email to rose@rose-rosetree.com or call 703-450-9514. Scheduling a personal session can only help you as a Skilled Empath.

4. GROUP STUDY

Classes are a great way to learn more about the joys of life as a Skilled Empath. Check the schedule of Intensives at www.rose-rosetree.com. I would love to meet you in person and be of service to you in this way.

But please don't wait for me to come to your neighborhood. The convenience of a McDonald's happens when something is very mainstream. Empath Empowerment is an emerging skill for the entire planet, so consider coming out to study with me!

And do remember that personal coaching will always be the most flexible option. Personal coaching plus .... this book and *Empowered by Empathy.*

5. MENTORING PROGRAM

f you are interested in depth study, consider the Mentoring Program in Energy Spirituality. It can prepare you to facilitate powerful healing for clients and your own self-care. Add this skill set to your existing healing abilities or help clients by using these skills alone.

In this Mentoring Program, you systematically develop your personal gift set and combine it with the synergistic power of all the following:

- Yes, you can become an expert aura reader as well as a Skilled Empath.
- Yes, cutting cords of attachment permanently is a skill set that you can learn to do with professional-level results.
- Yes, you can expertly detect and remove astral-level debris, such as psychic coercion and various types of astral entities.
- Yes, I can provide guidance as you do your first 50 sessions for clients as part of myMentoring Program in Energy Spirituality.

This apprentice-style sharing aims to help you benefit from my 39 years as a spiritual teacher and healer.

Contrary to what current mind-body-spirit culture might lead you to expect, you do not need to be clairvoyant, or have any flashy gifts whatsoever, in order to become a powerful emotional and spiritual healer. The gifts you were born with are plenty.

If you study with me, I will not train you to become like me. I will help you to become like you, using the skill sets of Energy Spirituality.

Come join me at the leading edge of the New Age. Send an inquiry to rose@rose-rosetree.com or by mail:

Mentoring Program in Energy Spirituality
116 Hillsdale Dr.
Sterling, VA 20164-1201

How to Order Rose's Books

It's easy to order these additional life-changing books.
Within the U.S. and Canada, call tollfree 24/7: 800-345-6665.
For secure ordering online,
including excellent service for international orders.
click on www.Rose-Rosetree.com.

Empowered by Empathy	$18.95
Empowered by Empathy, Audiobook	$49.95
Read People Deeper: Body Language + Face Reading + Auras	$14.95
Cut Cords of Attachment: *Heal Yourself and Others with Energy Spirituality*	$18.95
Aura Reading Through All Your Senses Celestial Perception Made Practical	$14.95
The Power of Face Reading	$18.95
Wrinkles Are God's Makeup: How You Can Find Meaning in Your Evolving Face	$19.95
The Roar of the Huntids (Novel for Empaths)	$23.95
Let Today Be a Holiday: 365 Ways to Co-Create with God	$18.95

Prices listed here are subject to change without notice.
Quantity discounts are available.
Contact Women's Intuition Worldwide, LLC

Rose Rosetree says, "Sure, go ahead and do the Magic Picture technique on me. Nobody can hide from a Skilled Empath."

In 2001, Rose published *Empowered by Empathy*, the first self-help book in English for empaths. Teaching internationally, Rose has continued to refine her method of Empath Empowerment. Learn more at www.rose-rosetree. com.

PRAISE FOR BOOKS BY ROSE ROSETREE

Empowered by Empathy

If you are aware that your empathy — whether for people, animals, the environment, or whatever — overwhelms you from time to time, by showing you how to harness your ability so it does not run off with you, Rose Rosetree's latest book, *Empowered by Empathy*, could save your life.

— Cynthia Yockey for Pathways Magazine

Read People Deeper:
Body Language + Face Reading + Auras

Rosetree, who has published more than three dozen self-help books in numerous languages, mostly under her own imprint, recently passed the 800-interview mark on the media circuit. In this book, she turns her attention to reading body language, facial expressions, and auras.

Readers can find advice on how to discern clues regarding another's chemical addictions, sexual stamina, intelligence, problem-solving ability, confidence, truthfulness, and capacity for jealousy or loyalty, among other traits. She also includes ten rules to guide healthy love relationships.

— Brandeis University Review

Cut Cords of Attachment:
Heal Yourself and Others with Energy Spirituality

Rose Rosetree created a "manual" for all energy workers to study and use. First of all, it gives concise explanations, as well as theories, of cutting energetic cords that would be most useful for those just entering the field.

For those that are already cutting cords, this book would a wonderful addition to the library of resources....

Cutting cords is not new; however, Rosetree's book is new. I am not aware of any other book on the market that gives theories on cutting cords, as well as how-to.

Personally, I practiced and trained others on cutting cords for over 20 years. Because of my background and experiences I had with my clients, I feel Rosetree's book is precise and accurate. "Cut Cords of Attachment" would certainly have been part of the curriculum if it was available while I was teaching classes.

— Irene Watson for Reader Views

Aura Reading Through All Your Senses

She encourages the reader to trust his/her own experiences and perceptions, gives the most complete, least confusing explanation of the chakras and how they work that I've ever seen, and discusses such techniques as toning, aromatherapy, and utilizing the energy of crystals to enhance aura readings, all in a down-to-earth, practical manner.

Although obviously aimed at the beginner, the book contains enough new insights, background information, and infrequently discussed sub-topics to keep even the best read and most adept practitioner interested and happy.

— Anna Deborah Ackner for Lightworks Magazine

The Roar of the Huntids (A Novel for Empaths)

This author writes from what she knows best. She is an empath herself. Her ability to describe the impacts of the trends she has chosen to use is uncanny. Her settings are richly crafted.... We scored this a solid four hearts (out of four possible hearts).

— Bob Spears for Heartland Reviews

The Power of Face Reading

Rosetree asserts — and she has demonstrated it in thousands of celebrity and other face readings since 1986 — that our faces reflect lessons learned over time. This author urges us to see faces with eyes of curiosity and compassion, rather than with the thoughtless derision that the culture of the "perfect celebrity face" unquestioningly accepts and perpetuates.

— Ceci Miller for BigMouthBookworm.com